Keep in touch!

A practical guide to help churches improve their communications

Peter Crumpler

Scripture Union
130 City Road, London EC1V 2NJ

© Peter Crumpler 1993

First published 1993

ISBN 0 86201 814 5

All rights reserved. No part of this publication may be reproduced, stored in a retrieval system, or transmitted, in any form or by any means, electronic, mechanical, photocopying, recording or otherwise, without the prior permission of Scripture Union.

The right of Peter Crumpler to be identified as author of this work has been asserted by him in accordance with the Copyright, Designs and Patents Act 1988.

British Library Cataloguing-in-Publication Data.
A catalogue record for this book is available from the British Library.

Cover and book design by Ross Advertising & Design Limited.
Phototypeset by Intype, London.

Printed and bound in Great Britain by Cox and Wyman Ltd, Reading.

Dedication

To Lin, Matthew, Sarah and Elizabeth for their patience and support while this book was being researched and written.

Contents

Foreword 6

Preface 7

1 More than just words 9

2 Get your message across 15

3 Listen to your audience 21

4 Opening the toolbox 29

5 The media 57

6 All the news – and more! 77

7 Inside the family circle 95

8 Keep in touch with the family 101

9 Putting it all together 125

10 The way ahead 135

11 Where to turn for help 147

Appendix I – Communications officer 154

Appendix II – Communications survey 157

Foreword

It is patently true that God cares about both the medium and the message. The Incarnation tells us that the Word became flesh. Not only does God want us to hear his Word, but decides to make it known in the most accessible way possible – in human form.

The Church's communication should also be accessible, not obscure, and human, not lost in technicality. This book contains a wealth of advice, which many a church would do well to listen to. In these media-minded days, the Church needs to follow the example of its Lord in taking infinite pains to get the message heard. I warmly commend these chapters.

John B Taylor, Bishop of St Albans

While the best publicity for a local church will always be the quality of life and witness of its members, its effectiveness in mission will be greatly enhanced if it follows the principles and methods contained in this book. With clarity and thoroughness Peter Crumpler has provided a comprehensive guide to improving local church communications both internally and externally. No church can fail to learn something new from these pages, and for many churches a careful reading and implementing of his proposals could revolutionise the way they relate to the communities they serve, and considerably increase their impact for Christ.

John Capon, Editor, The Baptist Times

Preface

The Church in Britain has a communications problem. It fails to communicate to most people, most of the time. It is seen as irrelevant, out-of-touch and old-fashioned, and churchgoing as a minority interest. Yet surveys show that many people still believe both in God and in a moral code. But these same people see no place in their lives for the Church.

For many, their only contact with the Church are stories they read in their newspapers or see on TV: disputes between bishops or 'vicar runs off with the Sunday School teacher'. Why, they reason, would they want to get involved with a Church like that?

Meanwhile, there are churches all over Britain with lively services and welcoming events wondering why their impact on the local area is so small. They want to communicate the Christian message in relevant, modern ways, and to reach the thousands of people who live around their church. The question is how?

This book aims to help local churches answer this question. It also offers practical advice on how to improve communication within the congregation. After all, only members who feel involved and motivated can effectively promote the church in their neighbourhood.

Ideas which work well in one church may not work in another. This guide aims to help churches of all denominations pick out those which work best for them – and encourage them to think up others.

Good communicating!

Acknowledgements

Special thanks to John Capon of the Baptist Union, Peter Meadows of Bridgehead Communications, John Truscott of Administry and David Denyer of Agape for their support and advice.

Thanks also to the numerous Christian organizations and people who have helped with ideas and examples. May their work be greatly blessed.

Funds from the sale of this book are going to support the work of the Shaftesbury Society, which runs schools, residential centres and mission centres, to help people with disability or social need in the UK.

CHAPTER ONE
More than just words

Now ... right now ... this very moment ... *you* are communicating.

There you are, glancing over this page in a bookshop, at a friend's house or packed into a crowded commuter train – and you are quietly communicating to the people around you. Without you speaking a word, on-lookers are receiving messages from you. Your clothes, the way you are standing, the expression on your face are all saying something.

If you find that hard to believe, put down the book and take a look at the people around you. What can you tell about them by studying their faces, their clothes, the newspaper they are carrying, their shopping bag or briefcase?

Of course, you could be wrong. The man in a pinstriped suit reading the *Financial Times* may not be an executive hurrying to his first meeting of the day. The woman with heavy shopping and a toddler in tow might not be a harassed mum returning from Tesco's. But you are probably not too far from the truth in your assessment of them.

Shop Around

Shops cannot afford to make mistakes. In your local shopping centre, communicating a wrong impression could mean lost sales. So shops are carefully designed to send messages about the goods on sale. Body Shop's green image is very different to Dixons' high-tech appeal, and their shops reinforce the message.

Big companies spend millions making sure their public face communicates the right message about themselves. Everything from stationery to the way the vans are painted, from shopfronts to staff uniforms all support 'the image'. For example, British Telecom dispensed with its familiar yellow vans and Telecom symbol for a colourful 'Pied Piper' style more in keeping with its desire to be seen as a modern dynamic company. British Petroleum subtly changed its style to make it more up-to-date and recognizable around the world.

Buildings communicate too. Supermarket chains, like Asda and Sainsbury's, give great importance to their appearances. They design their new buildings to be welcoming, distinctive – and clearly recognizable as shops. They know that buildings communicate, and a poorly-designed structure can deter customers from walking through the door (especially if they cannot find it!). Breweries invest in making pubs and clubs welcoming, inside and out, using colour schemes, design, lighting and other techniques.

The same principles that apply to superstores and pubs also apply to churches. What, for example, is your church building communicating to passers-by at this moment? Is its drab exterior communicating neglect and unconcern? Are its high walls warning local people to keep away? Or is it reaching out to the community with a welcoming frontage and bright appearance?

Communications are more than just words. Organizations communicate, buildings communicate and you communicate, without saying anything. But, when you do speak, you reveal a lot more about yourself ... and actions speak even louder.

A look at Jesus' example

Communication plays a vital role in any church's activities – from churches with hundreds of members in a leafy stockbroker belt, to small mission churches on inner city estates; from parish churches in rural areas, to fellowships meeting in the local primary school. The challenge to communicate effectively is the same for every church and every Christian – and it requires more than simply sticking up a text poster outside the church, or giving out evangelistic tracts.

We live in a world of complex communication, where everyone is bombarded with messages from the time they wake up with the morning radio show, till the time they fall asleep in front of the TV with the newspaper open on their lap. . . Local churches wanting to make an impact in their communities in the 1990s and beyond will need to:

- know what they want to communicate,
- know with whom they want to communicate,
- make sure the message is clearly received.

We can learn by looking at Jesus' example.

Jesus knew his message

'Turn away from your sins and believe the Good News!' preached Christ, right from the outset. He summed up his message in a headline sentence, then built on the theme in sermons and parables. He knew exactly what he wanted to say, and did not allow himself to be deflected or side-tracked from it. All his preaching and teaching combine to reinforce the central message of repentance and belief in himself as the Good News for the world.

Jesus knew his audience

Born among poor people, Jesus lived and worked among them, grew up within their society and the teachings of the Jewish religion. Jesus *knew* his audience and their culture very well, and how his message would be received by them. He knew how women and children were regarded in the society of that day. He knew who, like the tax-collectors and lepers, were regarded as outcasts. He knew the Pharisees' role, and how they were seen by the rest of the society. Most importantly, he knew how the people expected the Messiah to appear.

Jesus knew how to communicate

Whenever we see him preaching, we see Jesus communicating forcefully and effectively.

- *When preaching to crowds*, Jesus used parables and everyday examples from the world around him to convey his message. He spoke of family relationships, bread, seed, lights and camels – things his audience were familiar with. He knew where to go to speak to crowds, and was equally at home preaching in the open air or teaching in synagogues.
- *When teaching his disciples*, he explained the meanings of parables to them, and answered their questions.
- *When talking to individual people*, like the woman at the well, Nicodemus or the rich young man, he communicated powerfully and presented a challenging message aimed directly at them.

Jesus made full use of two-way communication – asking questions to check how his words were being received, and answering those posed to him by people he met. And, whether challenging the disciples – 'Who do you say I am?' – or facing tough questions about remarriage, the Sabbath or paying taxes, he always created opportunities to teach important truths.

He encouraged others to communicate too, sending his disciples out to preach the message, and enthusing them so much that they wrote down his words, for us to have them two thousand years later in the gospels.

Jesus matched his words with actions – healing, cleansing and feeding. His miracles demonstrated his power and reinforced his sermons, going beyond words alone to communicate his message.

Christians communicating today

Jesus' instruction to his followers is to communicate, but the well-meaning enthusiast who scrawls 'Jesus loves you' on a motorway bridge or plasters lamp-posts with text stickers is not communicating a message about divine love but about vandalism. The crime cancels out the message. The challenge for modern-day Christians is to obey our calling to be communicators of the gospel, and to keep open our lines of communication with Christ as we pray and study the Bible.

A bishop, interviewed on local radio about the Church's communications, made a point which stands as a cornerstone of this book. He said:

> *The Church is in the business of communications. After all, Christianity is all about enabling people to know the Good News of Jesus Christ. So communicating with people is critically important for the Church, and we are always trying to do it better.*
>
> *The best advertisement for the faith is the person who lives a consistently good life. The best communicator for the gospel is a dedicated and consistently good Christian witness.*

An Oxfordshire vicar echoed this sentiment when he told his local paper, 'The best advertising campaign in the world can't replace holding someone's hand, giving them a hug and telling them their life is still worth living.' Nothing beats personal communication. Nothing can take its place. The slickest advertising campaign, media event or church newsletter cannot beat the impact of one person sharing their faith with another, and living a radiant Christian life which backs up their testimony.

But well-managed communications *can* play an important part in making sure that vital personal contact takes place. A newspaper report about your church could raise interest and create a positive setting for personal conversations; the church newsletter can open doors to developing relationships with local families; a community survey can help bring the church closer to the people it wants to serve.

So, what *is* it that your church wants to communicate?

Take action

1 Make a study of the way Jesus communicated. Use the headings in the 'Jesus' example' section of this chapter as a starting point for a Bible study. Develop the themes with more examples.
2 Think back over all the communications you received yesterday. Include TV, radio, newspapers, personal conversations, letters, telephone calls and advertisements. Of which did you take the most notice, and why?

CHAPTER TWO
Get your message across

This chapter is placed in an Anglican setting, but would apply equally in a Baptist, Methodist, Pentecostal, house or any church...

The vicar was taken aback by the question. It had been on John's mind ever since he had been appointed St Mark's communications officer. So, as he chatted with the vicar after the family service, he raised it.

'What is it about St Mark's that you want me to communicate?' he asked. 'I mean, I know we want people to come to our services and outreach events, but is there something special we should be saying about our church?'

Michael, the vicar, began considering whether he had chosen the right person to do the job. John had been eager to volunteer when the church had decided to appoint someone responsible for communications. Now, after taking on the role, he came out with this strange question. After all, the answer was obvious.

Keeping his usual close look-out for newcomers, Michael replied, 'We want people to know about our church, so they'll come along and be attracted to the faith. It's as simple as that.'

This was the answer John had expected, and it took him straight into the next question he had rehearsed in his mind.

> 'Yes, Michael,' he smiled. 'I'm really looking forward to making St Mark's better known, but could I have some advice on just how we want to be regarded? I think this is what publicity people call having "an image."'
>
> Michael almost spluttered his coffee in surprise. The thought of St Mark's – or any church – having 'an image' was just one notch better than suggesting the vestry be hired out as a betting shop during the week!
>
> Now Michael **knew** he had picked the wrong person for the job...

Or had he? The idea of St Mark's having 'an image' should not have come as such a big surprise. After all, this 'image', or reputation, is simply the way an organization or company is viewed by the people it serves.

The decision by St Mark's to appoint a communications officer was a vital step forward in managing that 'image'. It signalled a commitment to improve its communications and was an important initiative by the church. Many other churches could benefit from taking such a decision. (See Appendix I for an outline job specification for a communications officer.) Like every major organization in the country, the 'Church' – all denominations taken together – has an image, and that affects how every local church in the country is viewed.

Ask most people for their view of one of Britain's major supermarket chains, shops, banks, telephone, gas or electricity companies, and you will receive a wide range of reactions. Some of the positive responses could include:

> I do all my shopping there, and they give really good service. They're nice, friendly people.
>
> My brother worked there for twenty-five years, and he's always saying what good employers they are.
>
> They really make you feel welcome when you walk through the door.

Some of the criticisms could include:

Their service is really appalling. They keep you hanging around for hours.

I had a terrible problem with them years ago. I don't care what they say about being friendly in their advertising, I'd never go back there.

Their staff just couldn't care less. When you go in, you feel that you're getting in their way!

Ask those same people for their view of the Church generally, and you will receive opinions based on direct contact or contact through friends, and the impressions they have gained of churches through the media.

Communications specialists say that we all 'filter' every message we receive during the day. We judge everything we are told by our own experiences. If someone says to me, 'Come to church – it's great!', my response is decided by a range of factors including past experiences of church and how far I trust the person offering the invitation.

So when, John, the communications officer, gets down to thinking about his church's contacts with the world outside, he will not be starting with a blank piece of paper. His audience already holds views about 'the Church', even if they have not passed through the door of one for years. These views could be formed by:

- having friends, family or work colleagues involved with a church,
- seeing or hearing church news or services in the media,
- going to Sunday School as a child,
- seeing how vicars are portrayed in TV 'soap operas' and documentaries,
- attending church weddings, funerals and christenings,
- passing the church on the way to work or the shops.

Any view they hold of churches generally will colour

what they think of your particular church. Just like a customer who receives bad service at one branch will think badly of a bank's entire network.

It is against this background that John was asking the vicar, 'How would you like St Mark's to be regarded by local people?' and 'What exactly do you want me to publicize about St Mark's?'

> John felt that Michael had not really understood what he was trying to ask, so he put it down to experience and an example of poor communication. He would make himself clearer next time he raised the subject.
>
> Later, John thought about St Mark's reputation in the area. He wrote down some of the words he would like local people to use about the church, if asked. He wrote quickly and in no particular order:
>
> | Christ-like | Like a family |
> | Welcoming | Relevant |
> | Friendly | Growing |
> | Lively | Worshipping |
> | Caring | Alive |
> | Involved | Sincere |
>
> John realized he had found the answer to his question himself. He knew how he would like the church to be regarded. He had identified the church's qualities and could now work to communicate them.
>
> From his own experience, when he joined three years ago, he knew St Mark's was welcoming and friendly. Also, the church was actively involved in various ways in the local community, and its services were modern and lively. He jotted down a sentence summing up how he wanted the church to be regarded:
>
> > St Mark's is a loving welcoming Christian fellowship, working in the local community.
>
> This would mean telling people outside the church

about:

- *its commitment to the Christian faith, to show exactly why the church exists, and the message it seeks to proclaim.*
- *activities demonstrating involvement with the local community, to show that it is not an organization set apart from the community's daily life, and is striving to play an active and caring role.*
- *special outreach services, to show that St Mark's encourages newcomers, and welcomes them into the church's life.*
- *news of activities showing life within the church, to demonstrate that it is a lively organization with activities for all ages.*
- *activities supporting other local churches and Christian organizations, to show that St Mark's is not 'exclusive' or set apart from the town's wider religious life, and seeks to work alongside other churches and groups.*

This, decided John, would be his 'Communications Plan'. These would be the key points about the church he would work to promote to the people in the area. He felt he was now almost ready for action.

But first, he wondered just how St Mark's really was regarded by people outside the church. There was only one way to find out...

Take action

1 Does your church have someone responsible for its communications? Maybe the role is split between several different people, each concerned with one area, such as publicity, the magazine, noticeboards, etc. Do you think there are any advantages in bringing these responsibilities together?

2 How would you like local people to regard your church? Make a list of the key words you would like

them to use to describe it.

3 One London mission church distilled its appeal down to four words – 'Your local family church' – which it placed on all outreach material. In Houston, Texas, a church describes itself as 'The Fellowship of Excitement'. Could you produce a similar phrase summing up the main appeal of your church?

4 Take another look at the headings which John, the communications officer, was going to use to promote his church. Would you have different headings for your church? List the activities you would place under each heading.

CHAPTER THREE
Listen to your audience

Who is it we are trying to communicate with? What are they like? What do they think of us?

These questions kept buzzing around in John's head. At times, he wondered why he was spending so much time thinking through his role. After all, it would be simple enough just to put up a new poster now and again, send out copies of the church magazine to the local paper, have some leaflets produced at Christmas and Easter.

But he wanted to do something more. He wanted to look long and hard at the church's communications and work out what they were really all about. He wanted to do the job properly.

After looking at the key messages about St Mark's he had identified, John started thinking about 'the audience' for those messages.

Mapping out the territory

John spread out a street map of his town on the kitchen table. On it he marked the borders of the parish. He identified this as the main outreach area of the church. Churches of other denominations, he recognized, would have their own way of marking out their 'patch' and some of these would cross over into others. This was not a problem as local churches were not in competition, and worked together on many outreach activities.

Within his church's catchment area, he marked the other main local buildings: schools, pubs, shops, old people's homes, the leisure centre, libraries, day centres, other churches. He sketched in the council estate and streets of private homes.

All this helped John form a picture of his audience. In the weeks ahead, he discussed the area with neighbours and friends. Some of the questions considered were:

What sort of people live locally? Is it a broad range of ages, or is there a concentration of certain age groups?

Where do people work, and where do they spend their free time?

Where are the places where the community comes together?

What is the ethnic mix?

How long do people usually stay in the area?

Of special help were people he knew who worked in the community, such as health visitors, teachers or doctors. A local councillor was particularly helpful and Michael, the vicar, knew the area well. The branch librarian sorted out some fascinating books on local history.

John found out what the most popular videos at the precinct store were and chatted with the newsagent about the sorts of papers people read. He learnt that the vast majority of local people read popular tabloid newspapers and so would be used to receiving their printed information in a non-wordy, highly visual format. He made a note to bear this in mind for the written material he produced.

> *The more 'research' John carried out, the more aware he was that the local community was not one group, but a wide range of smaller ones. These included:*
>
> | | |
> |---|---|
> | *The elderly* | *Single people* |
> | *Ethnic groups* | *Physically or mentally* |
> | *Teenagers* | *handicapped* |
> | *One-parent families* | *Young families* |
> | | *Children* |
>
> *At this point, he felt he knew a good deal about his audience, the people who lived locally, but nothing about how they felt about the Church generally and St Mark's in particular...*

Carrying out a local survey

Most people have a view of 'the Church', but many will not discuss their viewpoint unless specifically asked. If you carried out some 'opinion research' in your area, you could receive some surprising results.

Fran Beckett, who advises churches on setting up community schemes, gives a word of caution about carrying out a local survey. In *Called to Action* (Fount), she writes:

> *To attempt to do this may mean that we're on the receiving end of criticism. There will always be those who seek to condemn or find fault with the church generally. The reasons for this vary. However, it would be a useful exercise to attempt to find out whether your church is seen as a place of welcome and care. Is it a place of refuge? What sort of reputation does the church have? And do new people ever venture through the doors?*
>
> *How people see your church needs to be taken into consideration because it affects reactions and expectations of you as a group of Christians.*

So, suitably warned, how could you carry out a survey in

your area? Visiting local homes has the advantage of bringing you into direct contact with people on their doorsteps. Drop a note through their door a day or so before you call, so they know what you are doing. Avoid calling after dusk, as many people are nervous of late-callers.

If you carry out the survey near your local shops, you can attempt to gain a broad response from a wide range of ages. Remember to stress that the survey will take just two minutes, and avoid anyone in an obvious hurry. Your first question will need to be whether the person lives locally. If not, politely end the interview.

Questions to ask

Try to avoid identifying which church you represent at the outset of the survey, so the name of your church is not 'planted' in the mind of the person being questioned. Instead, you could say that you were carrying out the survey on behalf of 'a group of local Christians'. Your questions could include the following:

Have you attended any local churches?
If so, why (wedding, funeral, regular worship, etc.) and how often?
Of which local churches have you heard?
Have you heard of (list local churches)?
Can you say how you came to hear of this church?
Of which local church activities have you heard?
Which of the following words would you use to describe the church generally? (It may be simpler to have these written out clearly on a piece of card, and invite people to point to the words they would choose.)

Welcoming	Hypocritical
Modern	Boring
Old-fashioned	Lively
Sincere	Out-of-touch

Which other words would you use?
Would you use the same words to describe the local churches?

After completing the questions, make a point of thanking the person for taking part.

Recruiting a team

Pick a reasonable number of people you would like to see interviewed, say thirty or forty, and enlist the help of friends from the church to carry out the survey.

Consider inviting other local churches to take part, so that believers from a range of church backgrounds can be involved in the project. This can communicate an important message of 'working together' to local people, who often perceive the churches as arguing amongst themselves.

Remind the team that they are acting as ambassadors of the church, and will need to remain courteous and patient at all times – even when they strongly disagree with the opinions being voiced! They will also need to avoid prompting the people being interviewed with opinions of their own. It is important that the views of the people being interviewed are the ones that are recorded!

Analysing the responses

When you sit down with the completed questionnaires, you are likely to discover a whole range of responses. An opinion research expert may dismiss your survey as unscientific, say you need to speak to more people, and ask your questions in a more structured, analytical way. But what you have done is to test the temperature of local opinion about the church, maybe for the first time ever. Your findings – and your actions in response to them – may be some of the following.

- *No one has heard of any of the local churches.*
Action: Need for a concerted campaign to raise knowledge of their existence.
- *Everyone has heard of all the other churches, except yours!*
Action: Need for a special campaign to make people aware of *your* church, and how you complement the activities of the others. (And make a note to find out what communications methods the others are using!)
- *Most people know the churches exist, but have little knowledge of their activities.*
Action: Publicize specific activities which take place at the churches.
- *People know the churches exist and the activities they offer, but cannot see the attraction of going along.*
Action: Communicate information from existing churchgoers about why they attend.
- *Everyone knows all the churches exist, and are eager to visit them and join in their activities.*
Action: Take a well-earned rest, you are obviously communicating well . . . or did someone forge the replies?

More seriously, the survey could highlight specific causes of concern as you discover that actions speak louder than words. The posters proclaiming God's love displayed prominently outside your church may conflict with the uncaring way churchgoers park on a Sunday morning, or the noise made leaving the church late on midweek evenings. Those problems will need to be resolved before looking to your communications...

Where do we go from here?

When you carry out an opinion survey, make sure you communicate the results to the people involved. Write them up for the church magazine, make the results known to the other local churches and send them to the local media as a 'news release' (see page 63). Remember to add a comment from the church on the results, and the actions you are going to take! This publicity will help the people who took part feel that their time and responses were valued.

Using this information, you now have a feel for how local people view your church. You already know the type of information you would like to communicate to them. So now is the time to start making contact – and to open the toolbox. . .

Take action

1 How much do you know about your church's catchment area? Where would you draw the boundary lines? What do you know about the people who live within them?
2 If you had never attended a church service, what opinion would you have of churches? (This is, intentionally, a difficult question and shows how hard it can be to put ourselves in the place of people outside the Church.)
3 Look out for references to the Church in the media in the next week. How far do they give a true impression of church life?
4 Plan how you would carry out a survey of people's views of the churches in your area. Modify the questionnaire included in this chapter to suit your locality.

CHAPTER FOUR
Opening the toolbox

Good communication is about winning attention in a hectic, noisy marketplace. It is about getting the Christian message heard in a world where most people have little interest in the faith and are not waiting, open-mouthed with expectancy, for the Church to speak. To communicate effectively, we need to compete against an increasing barrage of conflicting messages. Every minute of every day we are bombarded with news, advertising, music and opinion.

In this chapter, we take a look at the publicity 'tools' which could help your church or Christian group be heard and noticed. Use the right tool in the right way at the right time, and you are communicating. Easy? Well, easy when you know which ones to choose and how to get the best out of them.

Bringing it all together

Before looking at each tool individually, give some thought to how they can be made to work together. Try to use one type of communication to reinforce another. Devise a design style which clearly identifies your church as the source of the newsletter, magazine, advertisement, poster or whatever publicity is issued by the church. Just as any shop or commercial company is identified by a 'logo' that appears on all publicity, design a style of your own and include this on all your materials. This works as a short-cut to help people recognize at a glance something which has come from your church.

Designing a logo is one of those subjects on which everyone has an opinion and on which endless time can be spent. Essentially a good logo is easily recognizable, simple in design and capable of being used in a wide range of settings, from posters to bookmarks, from stationery to newspaper advertisements. An example is given in Figure 4.1.

Fig. 4.1. Church logo. The church has, on occasion, separated the distinctive left section of the logo for use on anything requiring a smaller format, such as invitation or information cards. Used with permission of Bracknell Family Church.

Once you have chosen a logo and decided which styles of lettering work best with it, stick with the format. Use the logo and design style at every opportunity, and make it well-known in your locality.

Now for a look at 'the tools' one-by-one...

Leaflets

Never underrate leaflets as communication tools. They can publicize a wide range of events and activities, are generally cheap to produce, can be targeted very closely to your audience, and can easily be passed from person to person. Some of their most common uses include:
- publicizing a special event,
- introducing your church,
- welcoming newcomers to your church or area,
- encouraging prayer and support,
- introducing the faith,

- explaining a point of view, for example on Sunday trading or the occult.

Before starting work on a leaflet, ask yourself the following five key questions.

Why are we producing this leaflet?

Try and write down the answer in a sentence. For example, 'to give information about our special service in June' or 'to welcome visitors to our church'. If you find you have two or three conflicting reasons for wanting the leaflet, then maybe you are trying to achieve too much, and could end up confusing the reader. Consider producing separate leaflets.

Once you have in mind the reason for the leaflet, you can make sure that everything on it works towards achieving its purpose. You will be able to cut out irrelevant words and make the leaflet sharply focused. South Parade Baptist Church in Leeds, for example, scored a notable success with a leaflet produced to mark the cricket test match held at the nearby Headingly ground. The leaflet combined a quiz on cricket captains with an introduction to the Christian faith and an invitation to visit the church. By sending a birthday poem with a chocolate cake to veteran commentator Brian Johnston, the church even managed to gain a mention on the radio ball-by-ball commentary!

Who do we want to read it?

Is this a leaflet for your church members, or for churchgoers across the town, or for teenagers, or mums with small children or...? Identify your audience as closely as you can. Then, using the information you know about them, target the information. Put yourself in the place of the person reading the leaflet. Ask yourself: 'How would I react to receiving this?'

What information should we include?

Once you have considered the first two questions, this should be simple. Identify the information you want to communicate and set it out as simply as you can, avoiding complicated language or religious jargon. Try to use short sentences and as few words as possible.

Be clear about the action you want the reader to take, for example, 'phone Blankchester 12345 for more details', 'call in at the coffee morning on Thursdays', or 'pray for an outreach event'. It is easy for someone close to an event to leave out a vital piece of information, so ask someone not directly involved with the event or activity to double-check your draft.

How should the leaflet look?

Put five people in a room and you will have at least five different ideas about a leaflet's final design. It is best to leave decisions on the format to one person who is given responsibility for the project, consulting with any others involved – but accept that you cannot please everyone!

So, if you have been given the job of producing a leaflet, you will need to consider:

■ *Design and format.* Aim to make your leaflets and brochures as professional-looking as possible, within your budget and resources. Take a look at the leaflets that drop through your letterbox and compare them with the ones your church distributes. Remember you are competing with these other leaflets for people's attention. Spending a few extra pounds may make the difference between your leaflet being read or simply thrown away. And that would be a real waste of money.

Study commercially-produced leaflets for the way they present information. See how an eye-catching headline, puzzling question, or striking illustration or photo is used to gain the reader's attention; how this is followed

Fig. 4.2. Leaflet advertising church carol service (A4 size). Note the strong Christmas tree design in the way the typography is laid out. Designed by Gillard Bros. Graphics. Used with permission of Biggin Hill Christian Fellowship.

up by information which explains more about what is on offer; and how the reader is challenged to take action – to 'send off the coupon today!' This format can work just as well for churches and Christian groups. Have a look at the design of the wording in Figure 4.2 for a leaflet announcing a church carol service.

Producing 'the artwork', the material to be printed, can often cost as much or more than the printing itself.

The modern method of reducing costs is by using a 'desktop publishing' software package, which can be bought fairly cheaply for a home computer. A reasonably good quality computer printer is essential to make sure the artwork is of a standard to be reproduced.

These packages usually come with a supply of stock designs and illustrations, and changes can be made 'on screen' quickly and simply. You do not need to be a computer boffin to use one of these systems as their designers have gone to great lengths to make them 'user friendly'. Extra material can be bought on disk from a range of suppliers.

A risk with these systems is that they make designing leaflets, brochures and other materials look simple. Some newcomers to desktop publishing get so carried away with the technology that they use all kinds of typeface styles, lettering, headline sizes and column widths within one publication! This looks messy and communicates a very poor image. A desktop publishing package is best used by someone who has a knowledge of design, or is willing to learn! Books offering advice on good design are available from most local libraries, and several are included in chapter 11.

A more traditional method of producing publications is to use instant lettering, such as Letraset which can be bought in sheets, to emphasize headings and main points. The rest of the text can be produced on a word processor or typewriter. This can be fiddly and time-consuming and is fast being overtaken by desktop publishing.

A wide range of excellent 'instant art' books are also available, with a growing number specifically for church use. These are packed with illustrations and headings, which can be reproduced free of charge. The material can significantly improve the look of your publicity.

Overprinting a preprinted leaflet is usually much cheaper than producing a leaflet from scratch. It also gives you the option of using full colour printing at a fraction of the cost. Remember to include your church logo and to choose a lettering style which matches your other material, so that the overprinted leaflets reinforce the impact of your other church publicity.

The Christian Publicity Organisation leads the field in top-quality materials for use by local churches and groups. They have an extensive range of materials available, from invitations to welcome materials, bookmarks, posters and leaflets to introduce your church. CPO has also published helpful guidelines for churches who ask them to produce their publicity material:

> *Consider carefully who you want to reach with the brochure.*
>
> *Be clear what you want the readers to do after they have read it.*
>
> *Select the content with care, never losing sight of who your readers are and what you want them to do.*
>
> *Communicate politely! That means using words and images the reader understands and will enjoy.*
>
> *Always try to reduce the number of words; this invariably means you will have to leave some good material out.*
>
> *Choosing which photographs to include poses several important questions:*
>
> *Is it an attractive picture. Will it print?*
> *Is it in focus?*

Size doesn't matter, pictures can be enlarged or reduced, but the shape must be the same as the space in which it will be printed.
It can be a colour print, black and white print or 35 mm slide.

If drawings are supplied for inclusion, they must be black on white paper.
Size is not important, drawings can be enlarged or reduced, but the shape of the drawing must fit the shape in which it is to be printed.

If a map is required remember it is normally illegal to photocopy maps without prior copyright clearance.

- *Size.* Most leaflets are based on the common A4 size (210 mm × 297 mm). Sheets can be folded into three to give a leaflet that opens either horizontally or vertically. A4-size sheets can also be folded in half to A5 (148 mm × 210 mm), although A5 size is best kept for single sheet handbills. Straying outside standard paper sizes can sharply increase your printing costs.
- *Type of paper or card.* A standard cartridge paper will usually do, but you may want to invest in a thin card or a better quality paper for leaflets that are designed to be kept for a longer period. Use coloured paper to give your leaflets more appeal, with black (or another colour) lettering printed on a strong colour. Take care with tinted papers as these can convey a cheap, weak effect. Consider using recycled paper to demonstrate your church is caring for God's world, and add a note saying you have done so.
- *Quantity.* Resist the temptation to have thousands produced because of all the work you put into the leaflet. Calculate how many you need, and add 10 per cent for unexpected demands.

How will the leaflets be distributed?

Take time to consider how the leaflets will reach their readers. Will they be:
- handed to passers-by?
- dropped through letter boxes?
- delivered with one of the local free newspapers?
- given to people visited by church members?
- given to visitors to the church?
- left at local information centres and libraries?

Bear this in mind right from the outset of your thinking. After all, a leaflet that has to be picked up from among a library rack full of other publications has to work harder to be noticed than one dropped through the letterbox or given out by hand.

Work out the most effective way of using the leaflets and get them into use as quickly as possible. There is something particularly depressing about finding a pile of well-produced leaflets gathering dust in a corner of the church foyer.

A final word on leaflets. Used properly, leaflets can reinforce that vital person-to-person contact, which is the most effective form of communication. They can never replace it. Any church that suspects it may be distributing leaflets to avoid contacting people face to face could be missing out on real communication. . .

Newsletters

Most churches produce a publication for members, and many distribute or sell it to homes in the area. Far fewer take up the challenge to produce a newsletter solely aimed at people *outside* the church. A survey carried out by church administration specialists, Administry, in the mid-eighties found few churches venturing into this territory, and there is little to indicate that numbers have soared in the years since then.

Some readers may ask, 'Why bother? Couldn't we just

distribute our church magazine to local homes?' The answer, of course, is that you could, and for churches with few members it might be a good idea to combine the two. But, since the two types of publication have very different functions and audiences, this makes for an uneasy partnership. Tailor your messages to fit your different audiences, and you have more chance of hitting your target.

Like all forms of communication, the newsletter should be aimed carefully at its potential readership. What sort of publication do they usually read? What information about your church would interest them most? The newsletter needs to be short on words, with plenty of illustrations and information likely to interest the casual reader. It has to be able to pass the 'five second test' – will it be in the dustbin five seconds after dropping on the doormat?

There is no need to spend hundreds of pounds on sophisticated design and full-colour printing. Keep it simple and easy to read, with a friendly local feel to it. Like a neighbour dropping by, or a message from one group of local people to another. The contents could include:

- basic information on church activities,
- a short and relevant gospel message,
- a brief testimony from a local person,
- a telephone number for more information.

Place an eye-catching photograph, a cartoon or a striking headline on the front to catch the reader's attention. Highlight church activities like parent-and-toddler clubs, drop-ins or advice centres. Casual readers are more likely to call into these than church services. Consider adding information on other local services, such as the Citizen's Advice Bureau or residents group, to demonstrate you are part of the community. Resist the urge to include information on the flower rota or the deacons' meeting. Keep this type of material for the internal church publication.

If you produce the newsletter monthly or quarterly, it will regularly bring the church to the attention of local people. A consistent style – recognizable as from your church – will help reinforce the impact. The format of the newsletter can vary tremendously – from a single folded A4 sheet, like that delivered by Syon Mission Church in Brentford to a thousand local homes, to the tabloid newspaper produced by Southampton Community Church and distributed to thirty thousand homes in the area. Their *Ordinary People* publication includes testimonies of church members, gospel messages linked to topical events, and information on church activities. In a recent edition, a member's testimony was depicted as a strip-cartoon to make it easy to read. Paid advertising helps to keep the costs low, and distribution is carried out by church members.

When Acorn Church in Sidcup, Kent, acquired premises for the first time, it produced *Acorn News* to mark the opening and had the four-page, tabloid-style publication distributed across the area by a local newspaper. *Acorn News* told the story of the church and gave the testimonies of several church members. Prominently featured was a photograph of the church 'family' gathered outside the building.

The most well-known church outreach newspaper is the Salvation Army's *War Cry*. Launched in the 1870s, it maintains a high standard of design and impact, with topical stories and comment to catch the reader's eye. The Elim Pentecostal Church also produces a monthly colour magazine, *Direction*, as an outreach publication for its local churches. The Challenge Literature Fellowship produces an evangelistic newspaper *Challenge*, which churches can order in bulk for local distribution and overprint with local material.

Church brochures

The church brochure says more about your church than any other piece of printed material you produce. It is the leaflet or booklet that says, 'This is us – come and join us!' Most church brochures will include a welcome, a description of events and types of activities, location details, possibly a brief history, and some method of responding, such as a coupon to return, tear-off postcard or telephone number to ring. Figure 4.3 gives an excellent example of a church brochure aimed at readers who want to take in information at a glance.

Fig. 4.3. Church brochure, used with permission of Poplar & Berger Baptist Church in East London. Designed and printed by the Christian Publicity Organisation.

A brief testimony from a church member, avoiding religious jargon or cliches, can reinforce the message that 'local people like us' go to church.

A brochure's format will be as wide-ranging as the types of church. Examples that have passed across my desk recently include one featuring full colour photographs of popular tourist landmarks in the church's town; a booklet with artistic black-and-white photos showing different aspects of the church's life; and a third produced on duplicated paper with line drawings of the church building.

Whatever design you adopt, it is important that churchgoers feel 'comfortable' with the brochure. Otherwise, they are unlikely to show it to their friends. Sometimes it may be best to opt for a more 'traditional' design that will be widely used and accepted by all ages in the church, than something that will, say, only appeal to the youngsters. Most importantly, the brochure has to present the church as lively and relevant to people who currently do not attend.

Advertising

Effective advertising gets noticed. It wins attention and make people think about what is being advertised. We know what Beanz Meanz, what refreshes the parts other beers do not reach, and which fuel delivers cookability, thanks to the impact which advertising has made on our lives.

Charities with a wide appeal, like the Children's Society and Christian Aid make effective use of advertising, and professional campaigns for Billy Graham (L.I.F.E. – who can make sense of it?) and other evangelists have helped draw crowds to their meetings.

Increasingly, churches are combining their resources to buy newspaper and radio ads. The Oxford Diocese encouraged radio listeners at Christmas to 'Give your kids a treat. Wrap them up and bring them to church' and has since been experimenting with other advertising campaigns.

Changes in the rules on TV advertising mean that churches are free to buy space, though with some restrictions, and several experiments are under way to take advantage of the relaxation. At a local level, churches often combine to place advertisements at Christmas or Easter. In Hounslow, a London borough with a multi-ethnic population, the churches joined forces to advertise the Christmas message in dozens of languages spoken locally.

Many churches are deterred by the costs of advertising, yet it can be a cost-effective way of reaching large audiences, with a straightforward message. Places where you could advertise include:

- local newspapers and radio,
- directories,
- sports grounds,
- railway and bus stations,
- programmes of local groups, e.g. the drama club or horticultural society,
- your cinema!

Local newspapers and radio may give you a special rate because you are a voluntary group. Always negotiate with the sales representative as discounts are often available. A Midlands Assemblies of God pastor, who was quoted £1,200 for one full page ad, eventually paid £400 – and later discovered he could have bought the space for just £250!

Fellowships that do not have buildings of their own and meet, say in a local school or community hall, will need to work harder at making themselves known. A regular advertisement in the local newspaper is a good investment in publicity, linked to other methods outlined in this book.

Devise a common style for advertisements so that readers will easily recognize them. The advertising departments of the newspapers and radio will be happy to help you with this. Keep the layout simple with as few words as possible, and seek to communicate basic information about your church in a friendly way.

Local directories, such as *Yellow Pages* or *The Thomson Directory* are very popular with local tradespeople. They know that people reach for them when they are seeking a plumber, roof repairer or to hire a van. An advert here could attract people new to your area who are looking for a church.

Advertising at local sites where people gather, such as railway stations, bus garages and sports centres, is also worth considering, and special rates are usually available for long-term advertising, say, over a year. The Metropolitan Tabernacle, in London's Elephant & Castle, has placed cartoon-style ads on the Underground for many years. A church representative told me, 'We have found it a very useful method of bringing people to the church to hear the gospel, and people regularly come in because of it. It is an expensive way of advertising, but because it has been effective, we have kept it up.' More cheaply, paid cards in shop windows, and advertisements in the programmes of your local theatre group, sports group or horticultural society, are also worth following up.

Noticeboards and posters

Outside

Spare a thought for the noticeboard outside the church. There it stands, in the cold, the rain and the summer sun, proclaiming a message about your church. It is working as long as there is light to see it by – longer, if you have an illuminated board.

I have taken for granted that your noticeboard announces the church name and gives basic details of your main activities and church officers. I have assumed it looks bright and welcoming, and is not in need of a coat of paint, or in danger of being swamped by the church garden growing around it... But is it saying anything else?

> *Our board's empty, so it isn't communicating anything!*

That is what you think. To passers-by, the church noticeboard that is empty, except for any basic information, may be loudly proclaiming that this church has nothing to say.

> *How long halt ye between two opinions?*

A challenging Scripture text painted on the board, or on

a poster, demonstrates the church is seeking to communicate a gospel message. But the use of language from the seventeenth century can also communicate that the church is behind the times.

This Sunday's preacher: Rev. John Smith.

Unless you have Billy Graham as a visiting preacher, or the speaker is especially well-known locally, the name of your Sunday speaker is rarely going to draw a crowd. Could the space be used for something more appealing, such as the theme of the service? For example, 'How to find a purpose in life' or 'What Easter really means'.

Come to our Christmas services!

Great! Here is a church that wants to encourage people to come inside – except this poster was still up in the middle of March… Out-of-date, peeling posters communicate a lack of care and a slap-dash approach.

Seriously, noticeboards with space for posters are an asset to any church. If your church does not have one, act fast and have one installed. Check with the local council to see if planning permission is required. The investment is a good one as:

- *posters challenge passers-by with the Christian gospel.* By all means use Scripture verses – the Bible promises that God's word will always have an effect on people open to receiving it. If you use a modern translation, you will avoid passers-by having to decode the message to make sense of it. Another idea could be to vary Scripture posters with others which express a Christian truth but not in the form of a verse. A thought-provoking example from the time of the Gulf War read: 'Just War? Just Peace? Just Pray!'
- *posters invite local people to visit your church.* A simple 'Welcome to Our Church' poster announces that you are not a closed community and are keen to encourage people

to come and join you. Posters announcing special events and regular activities support the welcoming message. If you display posters that use the same design as leaflets you have distributed locally, you will reinforce their impact. It is a lesson to learn from TV advertisers who repeat their messages on billboards near shopping centres.

▪ *posters announce that your church is active and alive.* By choosing your posters carefully, and picking messages which have an appeal in your neighbourhood, you communicate that your church is alive and seeking to reach out into the community. The posters complement your other church outreach activities.

All this takes work, and you need to make sure your posters are changed regularly, as often as you like, but aim to ensure that no poster stays up longer than a few weeks. Keep a record of what you put up and when, and you will know when a change is due. Otherwise, those weeks just slip on by. . .

You also need to ensure that they are readable. Most posters are simply glanced at by people in a hurry, so they need to have few words and to communicate instantly. Only when the poster is by a bus stop, or near other places where people wait, can you afford the luxury of a few extra words. A good size is 508 cm/20 inches wide by 762 cm/30 inches deep, sometimes still known as 'double crown', with the metric size A2 (420 mm × 594 mm) as the next best.

There are several Christian suppliers of posters, including some in foreign languages for ethnic groups or tourists. Alternatively, someone in the church may be able to produce colourful posters to a high standard, or a local signwriter may be able to offer you a good price. See chapter 11 for details.

Your posters must be well presented, and there is a range of poster display boards available from commercial suppliers. The best ones are those that ensure the posters can be easily seen, conveniently changed, and well protected against vandals and graffiti artists. Boards with clear perspex fronts and backs that open easily to allow the posters to be changed are very popular. If the poster board can be illuminated, so much the better.

Whatever else you do with your noticeboard, keep it lively and changing. After all, it's the church's shop window! If you are looking to increase your impact, ask your local council if they have poster boards to rent. Some do, and make them available to local voluntary groups at low rates. Using a council board near your church to advertise your activities could add to your outreach at little extra cost.

Inside

Noticeboards inside the church play an important role in communications within the fellowship (this will be discussed in chapter 8). They can also help you reach people not involved in the life of the church. For example, if your building is hired to non-church groups during the week, which door do they use? It could be that more people enter by the side door during the week than ever come through the main entrance on a Sunday. If so, a well-placed noticeboard could welcome them and tell them about church activities.

Generally, posters displayed inside the church need not be as big as the ones outside, and can use more words. People passing by normally have more time to read them from closer-up. The A3 format is usually adequate to communicate a message. A range of gospel posters is available for purchase, or you can create your own.

If you produce posters to advertise a special event, then display these inside your church, as well as making use of them in other locations. Also, how about providing a general information noticeboard inside the church with details of local playgroups, doctors, advice agencies, etc., together with information about your church and other local churches? Suddenly your board could become indispensable reading.

Outdoor events

Using the 'great outdoors' can be a marvellous way of taking a message to people outside the church, and of helping them look at the Christian message in a new way. Planning, and paying great attention to how you look and sound is the key to success with outdoor events.

Open air services, street theatre and marches

These can be excellent ways of gathering a crowd and attracting attention, especially if you keep in mind the following points.

- *Choose your site carefully*, somewhere you can be seen and heard without thrusting yourself upon people or blocking their way. Avoid obscuring window displays and upsetting shopkeepers.
- *Make it obvious what you are doing*. With street theatre, you can do this with costumes and action; with a service, put up attractive boards announcing what is going on, and keep reminding people between songs.
- *Make it lively*. Illustrate any speaking with visual aids, make full use of better known and more lively songs or hymns, and avoid long sermons or speeches. Choose drama sketches that grab the attention of passing shoppers, not ones that require deep thought and intense concentration. Pay a visit to London's Covent Garden or other major cities to see how street entertainers attract a crowd. Sketchboards and other visual aids should be used to reinforce the visual impact of the message you are bringing.

- *Look happy*! If you preach about the joys of the gospel with a long face, the visual image cancels out the words. Smile as you give out the leaflets you have prepared for the occasion, introducing your church and your faith.
- *Make sure you get all the necessary permissions* from the local council, and inform the police and local shopkeepers about what you are doing.

The success of the March For Jesus events in recent years has demonstrated the impact and appeal of taking the gospel out on to the streets. People of all ages singing lively songs and marching through their area has proved a powerful way of communicating the Christian message. This is reinforced by the involvement and support of churches from a range of denominations. Again, it is the visual impact that is particularly important, whatever the type of march. Organizers need to encourage lots of colourful banners and signs, lots of people, lots of smiles.

Markets, fetes and car boot sales

Stalls can be set up at school, town or village fetes, or car boot sales, and are another way of helping to publicize your church, especially if you remember where you are. People expect to browse over the contents of a market stall or car boot table, so make sure you have something to sell, for example Third World goods or appealing Christian books, as well as material to give away about your church. You can also sell goods like these on your stall at a fete, or devise a game of skill with prizes, and donate your takings to a local charity.

Churches that organize their own fetes and jumble sales can use them as 'bridge builders' to make friends in the local community. Make sure that displays and information about the church are prominent among the tombola and hoop-la.

Carnival floats

These need a lot of planning, but taking part in your local town carnival puts you at the centre of your community, with exposure to crowds of local people in a relaxed frame of mind.

To make the best of your float, you will need to start working on it as soon as you have a theme, which is often provided by the carnival organizers. They can also put you in touch with local haulage firms to use one of their lorries for the event.

Carnival floats are the type of project where cooperation between local churches shares out the workload and demonstrates unity of purpose to the area. As with all outdoor events, make the float as attractive and lively as possible, with lots of smiling, waving people of all ages on board, and invitation leaflets to give away.

Open days

Fling wide the gates! Show you are not a secret, separate group by holding an open day at your church and letting people see what you get up to.

Make sure that something is happening for people to see. Unless your church is remarkable for its architecture, furnishings or history, you will need to stage activities to encourage people to drop in. These activities could include:

- displays of work by church groups of all ages,
- drama and singing,
- static displays and hands-on computer programs giving information about the church,
- games for the children,
- a welcome team from the church ready to greet visitors and show them around the displays or leave them free to browse,
- refreshments,
- showing a video about the church (see page 52),

- floral arrangements and displays – in many churches the annual Flower Festival is a popular attraction.

Successful open days need good publicity in advance, including leaflet delivery to all local homes, personal invitations given by churchgoers to their friends, and coverage in the media.

On the day, make sure the church looks like something special is happening, with a banner and balloons outside and posters in prominent positions. Why not invite the local Mayor and MP to come along? This gives the local press something extra to photograph and demonstrates your church's role in the community. (It may also give you the chance to bend your MP's ear on an important issue.)

If you do create a special exhibition introducing your church for your open day, consider leaving it on display – perhaps in an edited format – so that Sunday visitors to your church can learn more about you. Also, if a local group hires your hall for a public event, ask if you can put up a display about your church. You could try and fit in with the event's theme. How about 'Keep on track with St Mark's' for the model railway club's annual event!

Libraries and other centres

Take a look at a map of your area and work out where people regularly gather. Your research in chapter 3 will help you here. These are the places where you should be seeking to publicize your church.

Libraries and information centres offer a wide range of opportunities. Ask your local library to display on its noiceboard a poster advertising your location and service times. It may need to be quite small – A4 size or smaller – as space on library/information centre noticeboards is usually in great demand. Most libraries also have leaflet racks with information on council services, social services benefits and local groups. Ask the librarian if he or she would put some of your leaflets on display, and remember, from time to time, to call in and top up the stock. Many libraries and information centres mount regular exhibitions on local groups. Enquire about supplying one of these to feature your church.

Local councils keep comprehensive lists of all the local clubs and societies in their area. Many of these have been placed on computer for easy reference. Check at the local library or information centre that the details of your church are up-to-date.

Some libraries keep a diary of local events to which organizers can refer when planning activities. This helps to ensure their events do not clash with those of similar groups. Add in your events as soon as you have fixed the date.

Many shopkeepers will display small posters in their windows to advertise local events, including church activities. It is always a good idea if a regular customer makes the request!

You might also ask to use the noticeboards of health centres and hospitals to advertise playgroups, mother-and-toddler groups, drop-ins and other community-related activities. Make sure you gain the permission of the administrator.

Some schools have noticeboards which can be used for community purposes. Contact the head teacher or school secretary with a request to display material likely to be of interest to children and young people. Build contacts with the school Christian union where one exists.

Local museum curators like to keep in close touch with the community. If you are planning to celebrate a special anniversary, see if it is possible to have a display at the museum to mark the event. The curator will give you invaluable advice on the best way to present the information. If you are organizing a display at your church to mark the anniversary, ask the curator if you can borrow photographs or other items dating from the year when the church was founded. This helps to place the church in its historical context, and make the display 'live'. The curator will also be able to tell you what else happened locally in the year your church was established.

Remember to keep other churches and your local Christian bookshop informed of activities or special events aimed at believers, such as training days. Let them have a small poster to display, and a brief item for their church magazine.

Photography and video

The growing popularity of automatic focus cameras and video camcorders have made good quality photography and 'movies' widely available. High street film developing shops have speeded the turn-around on photography, while increasing numbers of young people are involved in media studies courses and have access to video editing facilities. So there are many ways in which you might use photography and video for external church publicity.

How about mounting a photographic display of the church? Bring people 'inside' your church by filling your outside posterboard with a display of photographs showing recent church activities. Or mount the display inside where visitors pass by. Be inventive, and have photographs enlarged to give them more impact. Have a really eye-catching photograph produced as a poster-size print, and watch it turn the heads of passers-by. Make sure the photos feature lots of people!

Peel-off stickers can now be made fairly cheaply from your photographs. An attractive colour photograph of your church (showing people, rather than the building, for more interest), could give extra impact to your newsletter or other outreach materials.

Encourage the youth group, or other volunteers, to

make a video about the church, and involve as many of the church groups as possible. Twenty minutes is probably long enough, with the momentum kept up by regularly changing the scene. Could the church music group provide the backing music? The video could be shown at a church open day, and copies made available to people considering joining the church.

See chapter 8 for information on using photography and video for internal communications, and chapter 5 for photography for use in local newspapers.

And there's more!

There are always new tools to be found in the toolbox. If this whirlwind guide has sparked you off with ideas of your own, it has served its purpose. You will gain experience by trying your hand with some of the ones you have not used before, and building up your knowledge of the ones you have. Here is a round-up of a few other tools.

- *Signposting*. Both the RAC and the AA operate a sign service for organizers of events. They charge for making and erecting the signs and obtaining local council approval, and need six weeks' notice of your event. The service is worth considering, especially for major events with visitors travelling from outside the local area.
- *Telephone message service*. Use a recorded tape to give a short message of comfort or challenge, with a further telephone number given for callers who want to speak to someone personally. A service can often be run by a group of local churches, working together.
- *Mugs, pens, coasters and tee-shirts*. These are just a few of the materials you can have specially produced with your church's name and design style. You can even have photographs of the church made up as jigsaw puzzles or coasters. These items can be handy for special events or for fund-raising, and they can also be a good way of

opening up a conversation about the church when friends visit a member's home.

Crusaders, the young people's organization, publishes a full-colour resource catalogue with mugs, tee-shirts, ties, key rings, car stickers – even teddies – emblazoned with the group's logo. Local leaders use the items for prizes, fund-raising and to publicize their group. Suppliers of a wide range of promotional items can be found in many religious publications and magazines like *Exchange & Mart*.

- *Welcome packs* produced by churches to welcome new people to the area. In Hampshire, for example, a group of local fellowships arranged for estate agents to distribute the packs to home-buyers. The pack included a map, bus timetable, information on local police and voluntary organizations, details of Sunday and weekday church events and a gospel.
- *Calendars and diaries*. Some churches distribute these in their local area. If used, they ensure that information on the church stays in people's homes throughout the year.
- *Car stickers* give church members a chance to show their allegiance to the church, or to publicize a local event. (Also known to improve the driving of churchgoers!)
- *Bookmarks* are useful to give away as reminders for prayer and regular interest.
- *Church bells* – probably the church publicity method with the longest history as the peal of the bells summons people to worship!

Take action

1 Carry out a survey of all the publicity materials currently produced by your church. List them and try to identify who they are seeking to reach. Are you producing too many types of publication, or not enough?

2 List the tools in this chapter which you have used in the last twelve months, and those which you have not used. Put reasons alongside your use/non-use of each, and consider if you are making the best use of your present resources. For example, would a transfer of time/money from one activity to another create more interest in your church?

3 What was the most successful publicity method you have used in the past two years? Why? How did you measure that success, and could you build upon it?

CHAPTER FIVE
The media

Now is the time to start thinking big. Instead of communicating with just a few hundred people living around your church, using the media gives you the chance to communicate with thousands, maybe tens or hundreds of thousands of people in your locality. Interested? Read on...

If you want to know about the power of TV, radio and the newspapers, ask a politician, pressure group or captain of industry. They spend endless hours and as much money as they can afford courting journalists and producers. They are well aware that a few minutes of airtime or a couple of inches in the press can make all the difference to their influence and standing. However, it is not just big business or MPs who can use the media to promote themselves. There are chances galore for local churches and Christian groups to make themselves better known.

Sadly, few churches take advantage of the opportunities on offer. One local editor told me, 'I hardly ever hear from the churches – they're very inward-looking.' A local radio religious producer lamented that, out of several hundred churches in his area, he heard regularly from about a dozen.

If the idea of appearing in print or talking on the radio seems alien to you, do not despair. Follow the step-by-step guide in this chapter, and you will soon be itching to feature in your local paper. 'Will this cost me lots of money?' you ask. In fact, it should cost you very little. This chapter will help you make a sustained effort to win space, free of charge, in the news columns and bulletins of whatever media is important to you. So, let us start with basics. The 'media' is a jargon term which includes the following:

- *National media*, e.g. TV, radio and newspapers, like BBC TV, Channel Four, Radio One, Classic FM, *The Sun* and *The Independent*.
- *Regional and local media*, e.g. Central TV, BBC Radio Norfolk, the *Western Daily Press* and the *Hampstead & Highgate Express*, plus growing numbers of community radio stations.
- *Consumer and leisure interest publications*, such as *Women's Own*, *TV Times* and *Angling Mail*.
- *Technical or specialist publications*, e.g. *Caterer & Hotelkeeper*, *Gas World* and *Baptist Times* plus thousands more covering almost every conceivable profession and trade.

Your biggest challenge is to know where to begin – and then to get started! Here are some hints to help you get up-and-running.

Getting to know the media

Find out which media cover your area. This should not be too difficult, as most libraries keep lists of the newspapers, radio and TV stations covering your locality. Local council information offices can also help. If a prepared list is not available, search out *Benns Media Directory* or *Willings Press Guide* in your local library's reference section. These handy books list all UK media. (It is well worth a browse just to see the wide range of magazines published!)

Then make your own list. Set out local media addresses, telephone/fax numbers, publication dates and the names of key staff, such as the editor, news editor and local district reporter. Make a quick phone call to their offices to check your information. Here is how an entry could look:

Blankchester Echo
14 St David's Street,
Blankchester, BK1 2KL.

Telephone (0123) 45678
Fax No. (0123) 45679

Publication day: *Friday*
Deadline: *Wednesday 4 p.m.*

Cost: *free*
Circulation: *60,000*

Editor: *John Kirkby*
News Editor: *Susan Slade*
Local district reporter: *none*

Content: *Primarily news of Blankchester and outlying villages. Likes community news.*

Your listing is just the beginning. The next step... Get to know your local media. Make those dry facts on your list come to life! How? Here are some ideas:

- Study copies of all the newspapers on your list over several weeks.
- Listen to the local radio stations at different times of the day and week.
- Watch the regional TV news bulletins.

All this is part of helping you find out which media will be most interested in news from your church, and what sort of news will excite them most! For example, it is usually much harder winning coverage on pop music stations with short news bulletins, on regional TV stations which cover a vast area, or in local papers which like to splash the latest lurid crimes across their pages and have little space for community-based news. So it may be easier, at least at first, to aim for the radio stations which give more time to news, phone-ins and other locally based material, and newspapers with more space for community news.

A word about 'Church News' columns. Some newspapers still publish these as a section devoted solely to items from the local churches. They are a mixed blessing. The column can mean that more church news is covered, but it also places the news in a 'ghetto' area of its own, read mainly by churchgoers. You are likely to win a larger readership if your material is published in the paper's main news pages.

Introduce yourself to each of the media on your list. If you can take along a news item with you, so much the better. Leave your name and telephone number with the newsdesk, and ask their advice on the type of news they like to carry. Take every opportunity to build your links with local journalists. Let them know about other news stories you come across, even if they are not about the church. Whenever possible, pop in with your news releases rather than post them, and send them a card at Christmas. Try and get to know one or two journalists at each newspaper or radio station and, as staff turnover tends to be high, be prepared to make new friends. A church correspondent in East Anglia found out his local newspaper group had a Christian Union and joined them at meetings.

Do not be nervous of journalists. They are generally friendly, eager to do a good job and, in most cases, younger than you would expect. If they see that you genuinely want to help, you will be a welcome voice on the telephone or caller to the office (except when a deadline looms). In Kent, a church member nervously visited her local newspaper office – and was promptly asked to become a village correspondent. Her role involved keeping the paper in touch with all activities from her locality, including the church news.

The growth of community radio stations will bring increasing opportunities for churches to become involved with local media. Up to thirty new local radio stations will be established each year during the 1990s. Already, some local churches are becoming involved in the teams running the radio stations. See chapter 10 for more information.

Getting into print

All journalists are hungry for material to interest their readers, listeners or viewers. The question is . . . what is news?

Start with a negative. The usual, the commonplace, the routine are not news. 'Church holds service' is not news. Neither is 'Vicar gives sermon'. But what about 'Church holds service in shopping centre' or 'Vicar speaks out against Sunday trading'? Now you have two potential news stories. Why? Because churches do not usually meet outside – or inside – Tesco's, and sermons in church normally avoid controversial political issues. Incidentally, 'Vicar speaks out *in favour* of Sunday trading' would probably attract even more coverage!

So, ask yourself, what news is there within your church? What is it about your church or fellowship that will win you coverage? To help you spot potential news stories, I have listed some possible ideas. The chances are you will have more of your own.

- *A missionary leaving to go abroad*. Definitely worth local paper coverage, and maybe a local radio interview. The story is even stronger if the person is flying out to one of the world's trouble spots. Remember to stress the missionary's local links.
- *A special speaker at a service or church meeting*. Maybe a prominent sports personality speaking about their faith, or the secretary of a national Christian organization or charity.
- *Special events*, for example children's holiday clubs, church camps, outings, holidays or weekend 'retreats', fetes, coffee mornings, jumble sales or charity lunches.

- *Special services* for Mother's Day, Easter, Harvest or Christmas. Try and find something different to say about your annual services. Maybe you are holding a march of witness on Good Friday, or sending a Christmas card to all the homes around the church.
- *A new extension to the church building* (or a move to a new one) – especially if it is because of your growing congregation!
- *A new activity or club*, maybe a drop-in centre, parent-and-toddler group or youth club.
- *An important anniversary* of the church or one of its groups.
- *Church fund-raising projects* or presentations to charity. Views vary on these. Some churches happily use media coverage to encourage public donations, usually for building repairs. Others shun this and also avoid coverage of donations made by the church. Each church will need to decide its policy. Generally, charities welcome publicity for donations made to them and will co-operate with a presentation. They see the coverage as reinforcing their promotional efforts. (In some cases, the publicity may be worth more to them than the donation!) Tear Fund produces guidelines for groups on winning media coverage.

  Ask your bank for a large presentation cheque in good time for the hand-over. This makes for a better photograph. If you regularly make presentations, consider producing a special large-size cheque prominently bearing your church's name.
- *Surveys*. These are good ways of winning coverage, especially when linked to some topical event, like Christmas:

  > *Four out of five Brentford and Chiswick shoppers agree that Christmas is too commercialized. This week, one of Chiswick's newest churches surveyed shoppers to find out if we have lost sight of the real meaning of Christmas.*

That was the opening paragraph of an article which appeared in a local paper in mid-December. It went on to give comments from the survey's organizer about the real meaning of Christmas. All it took was some time with a clipboard in the High Road . . . and the church submitting it as a news story to the local press.

Remember that information about events which are going to happen is usually more newsworthy than reports of activities which have already taken place, particularly for radio which likes to look ahead in its reporting. A parish information officer in Warwickshire discovered: 'The media are far more interested in what is going to happen than what has happened. The local press are very receptive and friendly.'

Writing a news release

All news items submitted for publication or broadcast should be presented as 'news releases' – a jargon name for a piece of paper with all the basic information presented in a logical sequence. If you set out the information and present it neatly, your news item is more likely to be reported accurately than if you try and communicate the details over the phone. It is also easier for the hard-pressed journalist to quickly scan a piece of paper rather than spend ten minutes on the phone gathering the details.

Sounds easy? But there is a catch. Every newspaper, radio and TV newsroom receives a pile of news releases each day. The challenge is to make yours stand out and catch the news editor's eye. Take a look at the example shown on page 64, and the key points which follow.

Marshalswick
Baptist Free Church

News Release

TODDLERS CELEBRATE 15TH BIRTHDAY!

A St Albans mother-and-toddler group will be celebrating their 15th birthday on Wednesday afternoon (October 31).

The Marshalswick Baptist Free Church group have organized a party with a special cake to mark the occasion at the Sherwood Avenue church.

Organizer Helen Little said: 'Several hundred toddlers and their mums have come to the club in the years it has been running. Despite many other changes in the neighbourhood, the need for clubs like ours remains just as strong as when we started.

'Mothers like to bring their children to play outside the home and to meet other mums experiencing the joys and problems of bringing up toddlers.'

Mary Brackenbury, one of the group's founders, said: 'When we started the club in October 1975, we had no idea how successful it would be.'

The mother-and-toddler group meets at Marshalswick Baptist Free Church every Wednesday afternoon at 2 p.m. during term time.

ENDS

Journalists and photographers are invited to come to the birthday party at 2 p.m. on Wednesday, October 31.

For more information, please contact John Simpson, publicity officer on St Albans XXXXX (home) or XXXXXXXXX (wk) or Helen Little on St Albans XXXXX.

October 15 1990.

Sherwood Avenue, St. Albans, Herts.

If you are now saying, 'I could have written that!', then the example achieved its goal. Writing a news release is straightforward, and the best ones are written in a simple style. To help you with your releases, here are a few basic tips.

■ *Use special 'News Release' stationery*, with your church's name prominently displayed, so journalists can easily recognize who sent it in. If you use bright coloured paper, it will help your release stand out from the rest of the editor's mail.

The only telephone numbers on the release should be those of people who know about the subject described. Avoid using stock church stationery which lists all the officers. If reporters need further information, the chances are they will phone any number on the paper. Do not waste their time by giving them numbers of people who cannot help. (You also risk annoying the church officers!)

■ *Type all your releases*. Beg, buy or borrow a typewriter or word processor. Handwritten news releases are prime candidates for the newsroom's rubbish bin. Type releases with double or one-and-half line spacing, and leave a wide margin.

■ *Think up a lively title* that tells the story and put it at the top of your release. It will help to catch the news editor's eye. Do not be disappointed if your (brilliant) title does not appear in print, nor if your release is reworded by the newspaper. Newspapers like to produce headlines and editorial in their own style.

■ *Include all the basic facts in your first paragraphs*. Answer When? Who? Where? Why? How? early in the release. Write in short sentences and keep paragraphs no longer than a few lines.

Speaking of 'When?', note that I have put 'October 31' in brackets so the newsdesk knows which Wednesday I mean – not so they will publish the full date.

■ *Decide what is the most interesting feature* of your news item and include this in the first paragraph. In the example, the idea of 'toddlers' celebrating their fifteenth birthday is the 'hook' to interest the journalists. If you are writing a report of a carol service where the Sunday school children stole the show, then make that your leading paragraph. Or the visiting speaker who brought a snake with him. . .

- *Use direct quotes.* A lively, relevant comment from a person involved in an event adds interest and helps the flow of the news item. If you want to express an opinion, do it in a quote. In the news release shown above, it is the organizer herself who explains that the club fulfils an important role. Scan the news columns of any newspaper, and you will see direct quotes featured in nearly every news story. By all means draft a quote for someone, but you must clear it with them before issuing the release. Include the person's full name and title. For example, 'Church treasurer, John Jackson. . .'

- *Steer clear of religious and church jargon.* The group's organizer could have said, 'We praise the Lord for his blessings outpoured upon this endeavour in His Name.' But this statement means nothing to the vast majority of newspaper readers, and is unlikely to have found its way into print. If you cannot find a way of translating a religious phrase into everyday English, leave it out. Also, do not assume that reporters will know what church terms like 'synod', 'baptistry' or 'diocese' mean. Always add a word of explanation.

- *Invite reporters and photographers* to come along to your special events or new activities. You can do this by adding an invitation at the foot of the release – as in the example – or writing a letter. If a photographer attends, a reporter may contact you afterwards for more details. Staffing levels on local newspapers and radio are very tight, so do not rely on reporters or photographers turning up. Be ready to supply a report, and a photograph (see page 69), immediately after the event.

- *Make sure you are available to answer follow-up questions* from the media during the day. Put both your home and work telephone numbers on the release.

Note that in the above news release I've added 'ENDS' at the end of the information submitted for publication. This clearly marks off the details added for the newsdesk only. This should ensure your telephone number does not inadvertently appear in print.

- *Keep the release to one sheet of A4 paper*, two at the very most. If journalists need more information, they will contact you. Type on one side of the paper only.
- *Date the release* to show when it was issued.
- *Check your information* with the organizers of the event *before* sending out the release. In some churches, the vicar or minister will also wish to agree the wording of the release. If not, let him or her have a copy as a courtesy. Journalists may contact them to ask about the event.
- *Post, fax or deliver the release in good time* to all the relevant media. 'Old news is no news' – it may be a cliché, but it is also true.

Remember that news releases are *not* evangelistic tracts. If you want to express a viewpoint, do so within direct quotes. No newspaper, radio or TV will allow preaching in its news unless it is attributed to someone, and it relates to a news story. On controversial issues, the media will want to balance any views expressed with those of someone holding an alternative viewpoint. Christian 'Comment' columns, which appear in some newspapers, are covered in chapter 6. So how did the toddlers' news release appear in print? Let's take a look at some of the coverage. . .

Notice how, in Figure 5.1, the Herts Advertiser has made few changes to the release, and used the direct quotes. The photographer took a picture of lots of lovely children's faces with a cake as a focal point. He kindly gave the church a spare copy of the print, which the Baptist Times also published.

Club's special day

A MUMS and toddlers club in St Albans celebrated its 15th birthday last week and a special cake marked the occasion.

Helen Little, club organiser at the Marshalswick Baptist Free Church, said: 'Many hundreds of toddlers and their mums have come to the club in the 15 years.

'Despite many other changes in the neighbourhood, the need for clubs like ours remains just as strong as when we started.

'Mothers like to bring their children to play outside the home and to meet other mums experiencing the joys and problems of bringing up toddlers.'

The group meets at the Sherwood Avenue church every Wednesday afternoon during term time at 2pm.

Fig. 5.1 From the *Herts Advertiser*, 9 November 1990.

Toddlers' 15th birthday!

LITTLE Grace Brown, two, joined other toddlers on Wednesday to celebrate a 15th birthday – of the Marshalswick Baptist Free Church toddlers club that is!

Grace and her mum Karen of Sherwood Avenue, St Albans, met up with nearly 50 other teeny ravers and their mums for slices of special birthday cake, balloons and stories to celebrate 15 years of the Sherwood Avenue club.

Founder Mary Brackenbury was at the celebration. She said she was surprised at the success of the club.

'When we started it in October 1975 we had no idea how successful it would be.'

The mother and toddler club meets at the church every Wednesday afternoon during term time at 2 pm.

Organiser Helen Little says although 15 years old there is still a need for the club.

'Several hundred toddlers and their mums have come to the club in the 15 years it has been running. Despite many other changes in the neighbourhood the need for clubs like ours remains just as strong as when we started.

'Mothers like to bring their children to play outside the home and to meet other mums experiencing the joys and problems of bringing up toddlers.'

Fig. 5.2 From the *St Albans Observer*, 7 November 1990.

> **A happy birthday**
>
> FIFTEEN years of mother and toddler togetherness was chalked up by Marshalswick Baptist Free Church yesterday.
>
> A special cake marked the occasion at the mother and toddler club, which began in 1975.
>
> Organiser Helen Little said: 'Several hundred toddlers and their mums have come to the club in the years it has been running.'
>
> The club meets at Marshalswick Free Baptist Church in Sherwood Avenue every Wednesday afternoon at 2pm in term time.

In Figure 5.2 the reporter has reworked the news release. This was also printed with an engaging photograph. Again, note the full use made of the quotes.

In Figure 5.3, the newspaper did not send a photographer, but used the key points from the release.

Fig. 5.3 From local newspaper 1 November 1990.

News photographs

Good photographs help your story to make an impact. A picture on the page draws the reader's eye to the news story next to it. The best are usually taken by a photographer from the newspaper itself, so always invite the newspapers to send a photographer to your special events.

- *If a photographer attends ...* treat them like royalty, Co-operate with the photographer from the moment he or she arrives on the scene. Your event is probably number four on a list of nine events to be covered that afternoon, and the photographer has minutes to sum up the scene and organize a lively photograph. Make sure the key people are available immediately, and give the photographer a clearly written note of their full names and titles.

■ *If not...* editorial staffs are small and many church events take place on Sundays, so you have to accept that the papers will often not send a photographer. In fact, in many areas, it has to be a major story to bring a photographer to the scene.

One way round this is for you to discuss the question with the local paper. What type of photograph will they accept from an outside contributor? Will they only accept black and white prints, or will they take colour prints with good contrasts for reproducing in colour or black and white? Auto-focus cameras have made taking sharp focus photos much easier in recent years, and one-hour developing services give a quick turnround to supply prints soon after an event. You can now buy black and white film, such as Ilford XP2, which can be put through the one-hour process.

Study the newspapers for the type of photograph they use. People make photographs. Always get people in your photos and avoid views of people's backs or pictures with people appearing as specks in the distance. An engaging photograph of two or three people involved in your event is more likely to be published than a view of a crowd of people standing around. Photos taken out-of-doors often result in better contrast, and pose fewer lighting problems for amateurs.

If you do not have anyone in your church who could take some standard photographs of the church leaders, consider investing in a session at a local commercial studio. You would then have some portrait photos to send to the press when issuing news items involving these people.

There is more to sending a photograph to the newspapers than popping it in an envelope. Your work is not finished yet! Whenever you send or deliver a photograph to the press, make sure you include a clearly typed caption identifying who is shown. In the case of groups, identify them left to right. Fix the caption to the back of the photograph using a light glue or sticky tape that allows the caption to be removed without damaging the photo. Use a hard-backed envelope to avoid the print being damaged in transit.

Do not delay sending in a news story because you are waiting for photographs to be developed or you are unsure which ones to send. If they arrive too late for publication, both the news item and your photos will be dumped in the bin...

Interviews

Good communication is two-way, so when you send information to the media, they may contact you to ask further questions. Take it as a healthy sign that they are interested in your material, although it can be daunting for church correspondents not used to answering journalists' questions. This section is called (rather grandly) 'Interviews' but all this means is explaining more about your news story to reporters.

Newspapers

When you issue a news release it is common for journalists to contact you for more information, usually by phone. In the case of newspaper reporters, this is generally to request more details or to double-check some point. Some newspapers ask follow-up questions so as to have a slightly different 'angle' on the story to their rivals. If a reporter phones you for a piece of basic information, like the date of your special event, then you have clearly slipped up. Put this down to experience. After all, you are unlikely to make this mistake twice!

Make sure you know as much as possible about the subject of your news release so you are ready to answer journalists' questions. If you do not know the answer, resist the urge to guess at it, but offer to find out the information and return the call – and do so, promptly.

Remember you are always 'on the record' when talking to a reporter. Be prepared to see whatever you say in print, or do not say it at all. That 'tongue in cheek' remark you made over the phone on Tuesday afternoon might not seem so funny in print on Friday's breakfast table.

Radio

All the points made in the 'Newspapers' section apply to radio journalists as well, although being interviewed for broadcast does pose some extra challenges. Radio journalists will usually ask questions based on the information in the news release. Some of the interview will be simply repeating the release's basic details for the listeners' benefit, but the reporter will often move on to further questions.

When a radio interview is conducted by telephone, the journalist usually calls you up and asks if you would agree to being interviewed on the phone. Then he or she switches the call to a studio line and records the item – normally no more than two or three minutes long. If time allows, and the item is not going out 'live', ask the reporter the main points he wants to cover and offer to call back in five minutes. That should give you enough time to collect your thoughts.

Interviews in the studio or via a 'remote' studio give better sound quality than 'down the phone' interviews, and are more likely to be used for longer items. If you are asked to go to the studio for a 'live' item, be prepared to be ushered in and find yourself 'on air' after the briefest of introductory chats with the presenter, often while a record is playing. To help the busy presenter, take along a card with your name written out clearly, and the name of the church or group you are representing. If there is a key point you would like to make, add this to the note as well as a prompt for the presenter.

A 'remote' studio is one which is unstaffed and could be some way from the main studio. You may have to open up the studio yourself and make contact with the main studio. (The BBC has a network of these hidden in the most unlikely places.) This sounds daunting, but is normally straightforward. For a 'live' item, it is also possible that a radio car, linked to the main studio will come to you. Again, this ensures better sound quality than a telephone interview, and is guaranteed to get the neighbours peeking from behind the net curtains.

If a reporter comes to see you or attends your event, he or she may bring a portable tape recorder with them and interview you while the event is going on.

Points to remember:

- *Be yourself*. Resist the urge to put on a different voice. It will slip and make you look daft. The best 'radio voice' is your own.
- *Know your subject*. If time allows, ask the reporter the sort of area he will cover in the questions, and make sure you have answers in mind. But do not write them down – nothing sounds worse than someone reading from a prepared script. I once sat in a studio listening to a police inspector read from a script as he answered questions. The case he was describing involved a frantic chase across the world for a notorious criminal . . . but it sounded like he was reading the telephone directory.
- *Keep your language as simple as possible*, and avoid jargon. Think of the interview as a conversation between you and an interested friend. Put feeling into your voice and sound enthusiastic about your subject. (If you are not, why should anyone else be!) Avoid long-winded jokes and wordy anecdotes. Airtime is precious and every word must count.
- *Think about the key points* you want to communicate and make sure your answers cover these points. For

example, if you were being interviewed about the mother-and-toddler club anniversary, (see page 64), you might want to stress that the club is:

- 15 years old,
- still in as great demand today as when it started,
- meets regularly (mention time, venue, etc.).

In recorded interviews, the reporter will usually let you go through your answers a second time if you 'dry up' or make a mistake. It is not in the reporter's interest to end up with an incoherent interview. In most cases, you have probably done better than you thought.

Television

All the points made for radio interviews apply for television too, but with the added vital caution that TV communicates *visual* images, far more effectively than words. This gives some extra points to consider.

- *Watch your body language and your eyes.* If you are being interviewed standing up, do not cross your arms – you will look defensive; keep your arms still, or you will look like an eccentric professor. If you are interviewed sitting down, sit in a comfortable upright position, leaning slightly towards the camera. This shows your interest in the questions.
- *Talk to the interviewer*, not the camera, and keep your eyes on the interviewer without letting them wander. Or you may look shifty.
- *Watch where the interview takes place.* If you are interviewed in your study with its rows of ancient-looking theological volumes, you may appear old-fashioned and out-of-touch. Why not be interviewed inside your modern church, especially if there is an interesting activity going on there at the same time?
- *Watch what you wear.* Look tidy and comfortable, but avoid wearing anything which could divert attention from

what you are saying. Avoid badges – they can be distracting.

Politicians and businesspeople invest lots of money to ensure they 'look good' on the box. Some church organizations also run courses to help their staff. I have outlined a few points to help you make, perhaps, just a few TV appearances in a lifetime. There are several helpful books outlined at the back of this book, for more regular 'performers'.

Two final words on TV and radio interviews. . .

KEEP COOL

You may think the interviewer is probing, adversorial, even aggressive. Usually he or she is only asking the questions which the people watching or listening at home have on their minds. So prepare for the interview by thinking about the sort of questions which could arise. Especially the one you hope they do not ask – it will probably be the first one!

Whatever you do, do not lose your temper, even if you feel your anger is totally justified. Showing anger loses you credibility with the listeners and viewers. They will forget what you said, and just remember that you got angry. . .

Take action

1 Make a review of your church activities and coming events, and identify a potential news story. Write it up as a news release, then take it along to a local newspaper for a comment on the story's news value. Be prepared to learn from their comments – and hopefully to see the story in print!
2 Look out for church news in your local newspaper and on local radio. What types of news win coverage? Make

contact with any churches that regularly appear in the media, and learn from their experience.

CHAPTER SIX
All the news – and more!

By now you should be fully equipped to win news coverage in your local newspapers and on local radio. No one is an expert and the more you work at it, the more you will know the type of material your local media will accept. Try to keep a record of all the news coverage you achieve and see what lessons you can learn by doing things differently now and then. A year from now you will be laughing at today's mistakes, and wondering why you ever despaired of winning regular coverage.

In this chapter, we look at other opportunities to win publicity through the media.

Features

What is a feature? In newspapers, it is an editorial article given fairly lengthy coverage, along with photographs. It may be linked to a news story, or can simply be an in-depth look at an interesting subject. On radio or TV, it is an item of several minutes or longer usually containing several interviews. Features are normally produced by staff journalists, sometimes in response to an idea sent in from outside. A phone call or a letter setting out the idea could be the starting point for a feature's production.

So there is the challenge. Have you any feature ideas in your church? Remember, they do not have to be hot news, but they do have to be interesting with good potential for photographs. Here are some ideas.

- A church activity, perhaps the youth group, tape library or Sunday school. There would have to be some 'hook' to catch the news editor's interest, such as the youth group doing something special; the tape library celebrating sending out its five hundredth tape overseas; or the Sunday school which is thriving because parents, even those from non-church backgrounds, want them to learn about the Christian faith.
- An overseas missionary. Use photographs and information to describe his/her daily life abroad, its challenges, and how the church back home keeps in touch.
- How the church maintains its links with a 'partner' church in a different part of the country, or abroad.
- How the church football team is the only one in the league which begins each match with prayer.
- The church project to take aid to Eastern Europe, or further afield, with photographs and a first-person report from one of the people involved. (Why not invite the newspaper to help raise support for the project, and have a journalist join the group on the expedition?)
- Some newspapers run regular features with subjects like 'A Day in the Life of. . .' or 'My Weekend' or 'Our Group'. Call up the newspaper and volunteer your church for a future column. Local radio sometimes broadcasts slots of this type.
- Special anniversaries. In chapter 5, I suggested these can make news stories. Here, I am suggesting something more substantial, particularly if the anniversary date is significant, e.g. 50, 100, 150 years; the church's history is interesting; and there are some lively-looking historic photographs available, with some potential for good modern ones.

Submit a feature idea to one reporter at a time. Journalists will be annoyed if they see a similar feature in a rival publication or radio station. Good times for feature ideas can be the summer and after Christmas when the flow of news tends to be slower.

Letters

The letters columns of today's local newspapers are like the market squares of years gone by. Everyone with something to say can stand up and say it and try to attract some interest. They tend to be full of letters from people with lists of points to make, often writing at length. Do not be put off by this! The best-read letters on the page are often the short ones making a pithy point. A successful letter for publication should:

- be brief – no more than 150 words,
- make one point – or two at the most
- be relevant,
- summarize any letter to which it is responding,
- avoid personal attacks, criticism or ridicule.

For example:

> *I was interested to read ('Comment Column', November 14) that Tesco's decision to open regularly on Sundays will 'bring some much-needed life into the town on Sundays'.*
>
> *There are seventeen churches of all denominations active in Blankchester on Sunday – and other days of the week – attracting congregations totalling more than 2,500.*
>
> *Most have thriving Sunday schools and youth groups and some are looking to expand to cope with their growing numbers.*
>
> *There is already abundant life on Sundays in Blankchester.*
>
> *JOHN SMITH*
> *Address*

The letter could have discussed the biblical case for opposing Sunday trading, or used religious language to describe the activities of the churches. Instead, it makes the clear point that Blankchester's churches are alive and thriving.

To help Christians make their viewpoint known in the media, the Evangelical Alliance's *Idea* magazine published guidelines on the content of letters. These advised the following:

1 Decide if the principles involved are debatable in the secular arena. Founding your debate on scripture will not make sense to the non-Christian, who is likely to view matters of faith as opinion and not objective truth.
2 Name the author, original article and date of publication (or broadcast) in your letter.
3 Check your reasoning is sound. Do not refute another's argument with subjective comment, e.g. 'No intelligent person could believe that.'
4 Be courteous. Your view will be less valid in the reader's mind if you are rude or disrespectful of other people's opinions.
5 Be positive where possible. If you agree with some points in the original article, say so.
6 Speak from your own experience where appropriate. If you can give personal examples illustrating the point you are writing about, you have given the reader provable evidence.

Why write to the papers? One Berkshire minister told me he considered it part of his role in the community to be involved in local issues, and to support this by letters to the papers. Subjects covered included the influx of office blocks into the town and the lack of activities for young people. Encourage church members who feel strongly about a local issue to write in as individuals, while there may be times for a letter from the church leadership adding more weight to a viewpoint. And do not overstay your welcome by writing every week on every subject. . .

In addition to the local press, radio stations include spots where listeners' letters are read on air, and TV stations include programmes like *Points of View* to make viewers' opinions known. The style of readers' letters in the national press reflects the paper's format, with the popular tabloids mostly featuring only brief, one or two paragraph letters. The larger the area covered by the media, the more difficult it is to get your letter published or broadcast. Yet, the chances are increased by following the points set out above.

Radio phone-ins

Phone-ins are the radio version of the local paper's letters' page. Since they were first introduced, they have become much faster and slicker, and the presenters more adept at getting the best out of callers. The programmes are a good way of winning coverage for a point of view, but you must have something to say; be able to defend your viewpoints and have answers to the main opposing views; and be able to express your views coherently and politely, including being able to politely disagree!

Listen to the programme a few times before you consider calling in, so you get to know the presenter's style and the programme's format. The advice on radio interviews in chapter 5 will also help.

Comment features

In newspapers

Comment columns are regular spots where local people can express their points of view. They can be written by readers invited to send in columns, selected key people from the community, or representatives of the town's churches. If your local paper publishes any of these columns, consider approaching them and asking to join the rota of contributors, if there is one, or simply send in a column. It all helps to show your church as part of the wider community.

The columns, published under headings like 'Speak Out', 'Public View' or similar, are places where you can climb 'on your soapbox', – but you do have to deserve to be read.

What should you write about? The key point is to think about what will grab the reader's attention, rather than what you would like to write about. Put yourself in the reader's place. Aim to make your columns:

- interesting and lively,
- simple,
- short and to the point (up to 500 words),
- relevant,
- topical,
- with a local 'angle' wherever possible.

Long wordy sermons are out. Religious jargon is out. Rambling meditations on obscure verses from the Old Testament are out-of-place. Think up an opening which grabs the readers' attention, and ideas that lead them gently from paragraph to paragraph, to your telling point at the end.

In St Albans, the 'Churches Together' group operates a rota of churchpeople who contribute columns to one of the main free newspapers. The week when an IRA bomb exploded in the city centre, a local minister linked the atrocity with his own experiences of people searching for peace. When the city's hospital was under threat of closure, another writer explained his feelings as he had taken part in a demonstration against the plan. In each column, a Christian perspective is given, but without assaulting the readers with verses and challenges about their spiritual state.

As the author of a comment column, you are a guest in the home of your readers, chatting to them across their breakfast tables. You have to win your welcome. A contributor to a Yorkshire newspaper's comment column told me:

> The variety of material which gets printed is pretty phenomenal, and some of the local laypeople are much more effective writers than the clergy.
>
> This may be because the clergy tend to move more in Christian circles, whereas laypeople in secular jobs are much more 'on the front line' and aware of the spiritual vacuum in the country.

On radio and TV

Some radio and TV stations also have comment slots, such as BBC Radio Four's *Thought for the Day*. If you listen to these regularly you will hear how the authors follow the type of rules outlined.

A Layman's Guide to 'Topical Thoughts', published by Grace Baptist Mission, contains much valuable advice on preparing radio talks. On approaching the message, it advises the would-be speaker:

> One person's experience is totally different from another's. Look for something that you might have in common with your listener, for example, love of sport, gardening, a mutual friend or acquaintance, children or topical issues.
>
> Always move from the Known to the Unknown, (that is, move from the opening which deals with subjects of mutual interest, to introduce the spiritual theme of your message).
>
> Keep a scrap book with anything which comes to mind about day to day issues, quotations, incidents, etc. that could be used as openings.

Other points to bear in mind are that the talk has to flow, read smoothly and take the exact amount of time allotted to it. Seconds of airtime are valuable. The script's author is normally invited to present the item. Contact the religious producer or station manager of your local radio or TV station to see if there are opportunities for you to become involved in 'message slots' of this type.

I asked an experienced religious broadcaster how he faced the challenge of being able to say something worthwhile in a minute or less. 'It's not so hard,' he replied. 'In everyday life, how long does it take to say "I'm sorry" or "I love you"?' (See also the sections on radio and TV interviews in chapter 5.)

'What's on' columns

Jumble sales, fetes, open days, car boot sales ... you will find them all in the 'What's On' columns of the local press. These are those helpful listings giving the basic details of events taking place in the coming week. Entries are usually published free for voluntary groups. Many feature special events only, while others are happy to publicize regular weekly events, like parent-and-toddler groups. A typical entry could be:

> *Tuesday January 6: Anyplace Baptist Church, Downby Road, Blankchester. Mother and Toddler Group. 2–5 p.m. Newcomers always welcome.*

Some newspapers publish coupons that have to be used to send in the information. If not, set out details in as logical a way as possible. The deadlines for these columns are often way ahead of publication, so watch out for any advice the newspaper publishes on how far ahead the information should be sent in. Newspapers that include regular events in their 'What's On' columns often expect you to fill in a coupon, or send in a letter for each week's entry. It is probably best to check the procedure with the newspaper directly.

If you are sending in a news release on a forthcoming event, do not take it for granted that it will also be featured in the 'Coming Events' column. You will probably need to send in a separate note or coupon to ensure the event is listed.

Local radio and TV stations also broadcast 'What's On' information, although pressure on these tends to be greater, with the station covering a much wider audience. Remember to send in your information on special events to both the general 'What's On' desk and the religious programme producer.

Specialized media

By now, you are probably buzzing with ideas for winning publicity in the media. Here are a few more for you to consider. . .

Hospital radio

In your contacts with the media, include your local hospital radio station. Staffed by a team of enthusiastic volunteers, its presenters are often on the look-out for interesting material between the records and requests. Your news releases could provide the basis for lively interviews and broadcast items.

You may also be able to get directly involved in the station's religious programme, volunteering to present a service 'on air' or give testimonies on the programme. Within the church, there may also be young people, and others, who would welcome the chance to get involved with the station on a regular basis. Hospital radio provides a good grounding in broadcasting, and can be both good fun . . . and hard work!

House journals

Most companies publish employee magazines or newspapers for their staff. Known as 'house journals', their editors are eager for news of employees involved in interesting activities outside of work, for example stories like:

> *'John Smith, assistant manager at Blanktown branch of SMT, will be spending his summer holidays under canvas with fifty teenagers...'*

This item in the *SMT Company Review* goes on to explain that John is the youth leader of his local church, and there are direct 'quotes' from John explaining his motivation in a publication that could reach thousands of colleagues and their families.

Encourage church members featured in the local press to forward a copy of the article to their company's house journal editor, or local correspondent.

Professional publications

Every profession and trade has its own publication, from *Farmers Weekly* to *Computing*, from *Accountancy Age* to publications for opticians, local government officers, the police and grocers. If you have a news story involving, say, an accountant going overseas to work for Tear Fund, or a farmer raising money for a local charity, send a copy to their professional publication. You will find the address in the *Benns Media Directory* at your local library. Good 'human interest' material is often used to balance the technical information which these publications feature.

The religious press

There is a wide range of general religious publications, as well as many long established denominational newspapers and magazines. All their editors welcome material likely to be of interest to churchgoers across the country or throughout the denomination. So, while the item giving the times of your Christmas services is unlikely to be published, news of some innovation at these services stands more chance of winning space.

These publications have small budgets and can seldom afford to hire photographers for local events. If the local press have taken a good picture of your special activity, obtain a copy from their photographic department and ask for permission to send it to the religious publication. Usually, they will be happy to grant permission, as long as the photograph caption says 'Photograph by Blankchester Gazette' or a similar wording that acknowledges the source.

Some religious newspapers, such as the *Church of England Newspaper*, also offer public relations services to churches and Christian groups.

Community newsletters

These publications are more local than the local press, perhaps covering only a village, a council ward, or a housing estate. They are usually produced by the local residents' association, tenants' group, or maybe the parish council. This may be exactly the area which you want to reach as your target audience. So keep in regular contact with the magazine's editor, perhaps taking a regular advertisement to help defray the costs, or sponsoring an edition from time to time.

You could even consider taking on the production of the magazine yourselves, especially if the present editorial team is flagging. In that way, you would be contributing to the life of the community and ensuring that your church, and other local churches, are seen at the centre of local life.

Questions people ask

So that was it! A lightning survey of other ways of achieving coverage outside the news columns or news bulletins of your local media. Now, the surgery is in session for some often-asked questions.

What do you do when the media make a mistake when covering your church activities?

Journalists are fallible. If the local media publishes or broadcasts something wrong about your church or group, you have several avenues of action, depending on the error made.

If the error is minor – for example a local paper spells the pastor's name wrong one week – then ignore it. Why risk souring your relationship with the newspaper for such a small mistake? (And are you sure your finger did not slip on the keyboard when producing the release?)

If the error is more serious, make an informal approach to the newspaper, point out what is wrong and explain the possible effect on the church. Most newspapers will correct the error in a subsequent edition. An example of this could be if a newspaper's 'What's On' column regularly publishes incorrect times for your Sunday services.

A third avenue is to write to the editor, requesting that the paper publishes a letter, an apology or a news story correcting the earlier item. This would be for incidents where the integrity or public standing of the church is brought into question. Journalists are seldom out to wilfully wrong any local group, and will usually print an item setting the record straight.

In the vast majority of cases, one of the first two options will usually be the best policy. The third will seldom be required. And if, for a tiny number of cases, satisfaction has not been achieved even after the third option, then the church should make an approach to the Press Complaints Commission.

How can you handle negative coverage? Our local paper ran an article criticizing our church. What can we do?

Occasionally, newspapers publish articles about local churches which upset the members and cause them to feel that the press is 'out to get them'. If you are active in your community, you could attract criticism. Criticism equals controversy – and there is nothing the media likes more than a lively argument.

So how do you react when the media produce a negative, attacking article about your church? The most important question to ask is the most simple: is it true? There is a long-standing tradition of shooting the messenger who delivers bad news, but it seldom changes the truth of the situation. Here is a (fictional) example:

ANGRY RESIDENTS ATTACK CHURCH YOUTH GROUP

Local residents called on St Paul's church, Blanktown, to close its youth club after noise from the club caused a series of complaints to the police on Friday evening.

Police officers who went to the club faced abuse from youths after they intervened to stop fighting in the church hall at 11.30 p.m.

Nearby resident George Sinclair said: 'It's time the club was closed. We've had nothing but trouble since the church opened its doors to all the local trouble-makers. It used to be nice and quiet around here before that new vicar arrived.'

A police spokesman said: 'No arrests were made, and the youngsters left the building quietly after we had made our presence felt. We shall be talking to the church about the incident, and would hope that there is no recurrence of it.'

The vicar of St Paul's, Rev. John Brown, who joined the church six months ago, declined to comment on the incident when approached by the Gazette.

Maybe if the vicar had spoken to the Gazette, he could have:
- apologized to the local people for the disturbance,
- explained that he would be taking steps to ensure better order was kept at the club in future,

- made the point that there was little for young people to do in the evenings in Blanktown, and the club had been started to keep the teenagers out of trouble.

Following the appearance of the above news story, the vicar could send a letter for publication to the Gazette explaining his point of view, but this would extend the coverage to another week's newspaper. It could also give rise to a continuing correspondence. It is always worthwhile for the church to be open in its communications, to speak to the media – and local people – and explain its viewpoint when *first* approached by a journalist.

If you have been winning regular positive coverage of your activities, then the journalists will know you already, and the readers will be able to place any 'negative coverage within a framework of your other publicity. The media is seldom 'out to get' any church group, but it will report the genuine concerns and complaints of local people, where they exist. The best way to neutralize the chances of negative media coverage is to address the root of the problem. In the example given above, the problem does not lie with the media, who were merely reporting the incident. It lies with the youth club, or maybe the church's relationship with the local residents.

Planning ahead can also be a way of avoiding negative coverage. Look ahead to spot any possible media problems because of actions taken by the church or its members. An example of this could be, say, if a church decided to stop hiring its premises to a drama group because it intended to stage a production featuring occult practices. Write down the key points you would make to any journalist who asks about the situation, and keep this handy in case of any enquiries.

In especially difficult situations, put together a brief 'carefully worded statement'. It could be that you will never need to use it, but it is best to be prepared rather than have to scratch around for a reply at the last minute or – worse still – have to make 'no comment'. The type of extreme situation where this method would be useful includes the treasurer running off with the church funds, the vicar running off with the curate's wife or the minister being dismissed.

We've tried for months but we can't win coverage in our papers. They just do not seem interested in church news. What can we do?

'What do we have to do to get more coverage in your newspaper?' a church publicity officer asked a local newspaper editor one day. That night, the church was burnt down by vandals, and the attack was the lead story in the following week's paper. . .

That is a true story. Of course, the publicity officer's question and the fire were in no way connected. But some readers may wonder to what lengths they have to go to achieve coverage. This is especially true in some urban areas where the local papers style themselves on the *Daily Mirror* or *The Sun*, and like to put the emphasis on crime stories, court cases or rows from the local council chamber. For them, this makes sense. In an area with a floating population and little community spirit, editors attract readers by using eye-catching headlines, with hard-hitting human interest stories.

So, you will have to put extra effort into achieving coverage, and you may have to accept a lower level of exposure than churches with more community-based newspapers. In addition to the points set out in chapter 5, the following advice may be useful:

■ *Demonstrate your involvement in the community*. If your church is seeking to remedy some of the problems facing the area, then look for opportunities to publicize the role and to attract more local support. Churches seeking to improve their locality are more likely to win positive coverage than those that remain set apart, following their own 'religious agenda.'

- *Look for the 'people angle' in your material.* This is important for all material sent to the media, but vital where you face tough competititon for space. Make a point of seeking out stories about individuals from your church doing something newsworthy.
- *Think about photographs.* If you can send in a good, eye-catching photograph with a brief caption, it stands a better chance of publication than a wordy release.
- *Be willing to be controversial.* Use the letters page to make points on behalf of the church, and become involved in some of the local issues that concern the newspaper.
- *Work harder at building links with the media.* Can you help with their annual charity appeal, if they have one? Look for other ways of getting to know individual journalists.
- *Be pleased with what you do get.* After all, it is the one or two-paragraph items that people read first!

Remember, like the publicity officer who asked the local editor about coverage, do not be afraid to tell the newspaper that you want to win coverage but you are not sure how. Listen to any advice they give and place it alongside the points set out above.

What about television or the national press?

All regional TV companies and BBC regions have 'local' news programmes, which are constantly seeking material. They are interested in news or feature ideas that are visual – or can be made so – and that are likely to interest a wider audience than the local radio or newspapers. Each of the TV regions covers very wide areas and needs material of interest to viewers many miles apart.

If you think your church is doing something very

visual, give the TV station's newsdesk a call, preferably a few days ahead of the event. Perhaps your vicar is climbing the church spire for charity, or chaining himself to the town hall steps to focus attention on the plight of prisoners of conscience. The TV station may be interested.

Much of the same applies to the national press, with the added dimension that the type of news which interests the *Financial Times* may not interest *The Sun*. A good way into the national press may be through the local newspaper journalist who acts as a correspondent for them, or perhaps via a local news agency (an organization which 'sells' news to a wide range of media). The national or regional office of your denomination may be able to offer some advice on how to make the best use of a possible national story.

Take action

1 Make a study of your church's special events and activities, and look for any that could make for a radio or newspaper feature. Try and summarize the idea in 100 words, and identify some possible photograph or interview ideas. Then try the idea on the newsdesk of your local newspaper or radio station.

2 Experiment with writing a comment column or a letter for publication. Sketch out the main points you want to make before putting pen to paper. Then remove any unnecessary words. See how few words you can use to make your viewpoint clear.

3 How well do you know the religious press, especially your own denominational publication? If you have not read it for a while, the chances are that it has changed significantly. Does your church have a responsibility to support a lively religious press? If so, how could this be done?

CHAPTER SEVEN
Inside the family circle

The view from the pew...

'Don't ask me what's going on – I only worship here!'

'How would I know, I'm not in the "inner circle"...'

'No one ever tells me anything...'

Grumblings after the service, hushed whispers in the pews, conversations that die as members of the church leadership pass by – all signs of a fellowship with serious communication problems. If no one tells you what is happening, it is difficult to feel part of a church. You see yourself as an outsider, not involved in the main life of the fellowship, even if you have been worshipping there for decades. As one church growth specialist wrote: 'Churches tend to operate on the mystery tour principle. The coach driver is the only one aware of the route...'

... and from the pulpit.

Church leaders often lament that attendances at church members' or business meetings are poor, and it is hard work to get people to stand for the diaconate or PCC. The only time they get any feedback on their leadership is if their sermons go on too long or services run late.

Seen from the church leadership's viewpoint, there is nothing worse than trying to communicate with people who do not seem to be paying attention. Whatever you tell them, they misunderstand it or forget. All your efforts to communicate come to no avail. Sometimes you wonder why you bothered to try...

Communication at work

So there we have it – two sides of a problem. A congregation that does not feel fully involved and a leadership trying their best, but failing in their attempts to communicate. It is a challenge many commercial organizations have been tackling for decades. Major companies spend hundreds of thousands of pounds trying to keep their employees informed about key issues. Some, like British Gas, have even paid for special TV advertisements and asked their employees to tune in. The vast majority of firms produce newspapers and magazines for their staff, and have them distributed at work or mailed to employees' homes where other family members can also read them. Other techniques include videos, briefing groups at work, and meetings where senior managers discuss policy and answer questions from the staff.

These companies regard the money they spend on internal communication as an investment. Every member of a company's workforce is a potential ambassador for the firm. Anita Roddick, founder of the Body Shop, summed up the feeling of many business leaders: 'Good communication continues to be the one vital ingredient in the success of my company. If that communication is honest, passionate and carried out at every level, it is a powerful force.'

A survey by market research organization, MORI, into employee involvement at work concluded:

> *Employers who communicate with and involve their employees and provide them with satisfying jobs are rewarded by a more highly motivated workforce, greater commitment to the business and support for its management.*
>
> *Committed employees work harder, come up with*

> *ideas that the business can develop, and promote the organization to outsiders.*

Replace 'employee' with 'churchgoer' and there is a message for any church leadership which gives a low priority to good internal communication.

Is it worth the effort?

Keeping the church family informed and motivated is hard work, and especially so because it is a long-term activity. You cannot communicate once, then move on to some other job on your 'to do' list. However, if successful, good communication can make church members feel:

- *more involved.*

> *Maureen did not realize the youth group needed a new helper until the vicar announced it in the morning service. 'Why didn't you mention it before?' she asked him on her way to speak to the youth leader. The vicar resisted the urge to point out there had been a notice on the board for weeks, and the vacancy had been in the church magazine for several months. Maureen proved well suited for the role, and it helped her become more involved in the church's activities.*

- *more committed.*

> *John had attended Freetown Evangelical for about a year before a deacon took him aside and challenged him to become involved in the men's group. He felt that John would gain from the fellowship of the other men. John's response surprised the deacon. 'I never realized the group was open to everyone. I'd seen the mention in the news-sheet each week, but thought that was just for existing members. No one had ever invited me along.' Soon John was one of the group's most enthusiastic members. He made a point of personally inviting many new members to come to the*

> group, particularly the husbands of women already
> committed to the church.

- *more motivated to support the church.*

> It was not until the church's financial position was
> spelt out with basic drawings and a simple format
> that Emily understood how much the church was in
> need of long-term funds. She had felt God speaking
> to her about financial commitment, and realized she
> should not put off the decision on a covenant any
> longer. 'I didn't think the church needed the money,'
> she told a puzzled treasurer.

- *more like a family.*

> Matthew was fascinated by the article in the church
> magazine on the Johnson family. He had seen them
> in church often enough, but had never really got to
> know them. Now he found out that Clive Johnson was
> in the same business as him, and their children went
> to the same school. He must have a word with him
> after the morning service... When, six months later,
> Matthew was made redundant, it was his friendship
> with Clive that helped him cope with the feeling of
> rejection and plan a change of course.

The five key themes

> Communicating with the church family is so vital it is
> worth devoting time and energy to making sure the job
> is done properly.

The case studies just given show the importance and benefit of good communication, and if the quotation above was on a petition, most church leaders would sign it without a second thought. But how many churches have taken a close look at how they communicate to their congregation? Very few, according to a survey carried out among a group of churches by church administration specialists, Administry, in 1991. They reported, 'Barely a quarter of our respondents claimed to have conducted any sort of review of their communications in the past few years. Of those who had, few had positive results to share, and some discussions appeared to have fizzled out.'

What is it we want to communicate anyway? Without knowing this, how do we know how well we are doing? In most churches, the five key themes for communication are likely to be:

1 *Teaching about the faith*.
Objective: to encourage spiritual growth in the fellowship, individually and as a group of believers.
2 *Discussions about the church's future role and strategy*.
Objective: to encourage churchgoers to be involved in the discussions. The more people are involved in shaping the church's direction, the more likely that the final strategy will reflect their views and win their commitment.
3 *Information about church activities*.
Objective: to encourage the church family to support events and activities by attending, praying, giving and playing an active part, including inviting their friends.
4 *News of people within the church*.
Objective: to encourage members to identify with others in the church family, feel part of it and share each other's sorrows and joys.
5 *News of other local churches, the denomination, and organizations with which the church has links*.
Objective: to strengthen the vision of being part of a larger church family which extends beyond the local church to churches across the town, the country and the world. To encourage interest and support of a wide range of Christian organizations and activities.

When you look at these themes, you see that communication within the church family is not simply an 'added extra' to the church's activities. It is vital to its efficient functioning and growth. Good communication could make the difference between a person playing a key role in the church's life, or remaining on the fringe, unaware of the opportunity to serve. The efficiency of a church's communication could determine the level of involvement and commitment felt by its members, and so affect its outreach and influence in the area it wants to serve. A church wanting to build contacts with the world outside needs first to ensure it is communicating to its membership and congregation so they feel fully involved in forming those links. Otherwise, the church runs the risk of 'outreach', 'evangelism' or even 'community involvement' being seen as the responsibility of the chosen few, rather than everyone's calling.

Of course, there are always some people who want to know everything and will never admit to having received enough information on a subject. The challenge lies in striking a balance so that everyone knows all they need to know so as to play an effective part in the church's life, without burying them in paperwork.

How can churches check their communications to see if they are effective? Just like a car has an MOT every year, and businesses call in the auditors, the next chapter is designed as a 'communications audit' to help you discover how well your church is keeping 'the family' informed.

CHAPTER EIGHT
Keep in touch with the family

This chapter is aimed at helping you take a look at the range of communications used by most churches today. It includes questions designed to help you think through your communications audit.

Recent years have given birth to a new breed of consultant. At a price, they offer to carry out a complete review of an organization's communications and come up with ideas for improving them. Their methods are hardly revolutionary, and can be applied just as easily to the smallest mission church, as to a large multi-national corporation.

Put simply, these consultants talk to people. They speak to senior management, supervisors, shopfloor workers, people who have been with the firm for forty years and apprentices who have just joined. They build up a picture of the organization and how well communications flow within it.

Leading companies take note of what these surveys tell them about themselves. Many are committed to following the advice of Lord Sieff of Marks and Spencer about 'the need to close the gap between management's knowledge based on experience and access to information, and what staff believe, sometimes wrongly, without the benefit of this knowledge'. That 'information gap' can occur in churches just as easily as big business.

Carrying out a communications audit

A communications audit for your church is not something that requires a doctorate in media studies or research to carry out. It is a survey which sets out to answer two key questions: 'How well informed and involved do people feel within the church?' and 'How could the church improve its communications?' It looks at all types of communication, from the church magazine to announcements in services, noticeboards and leaflets, and it seeks to assess their effectiveness. To plan your communications audit, use the 'D.A.R.E.D.' approach (as in, 'they dared to carry out an audit'!).

Decide

Take the decision within your church's governing system to carry out the survey. It is important that the idea has the full support of the leadership and has been talked through as an important church decision. Make sure that the church as a whole is carrying out the survey into its communication, not just one or two people within the church who think it would be a good idea.

Announce

Ensure everyone within the church community knows that the survey is going to be carried out, and that they will have the opportunity of taking part and being heard. Publicize the audit using all your existing communications channels. Ensure that the church leadership are shown to be giving it every support and explaining the thinking behind the survey.

Research

The simplest way to find out if communications are working in a church is to ask the people who worship there. So talk to them, either individually or in small groups, or issue a questionnaire and carry out a cross-section of follow-up interviews. An outline questionnaire is included in Appendix II. Make sure that the views of all groupings (age, sex, background) within your church are taken into account.

Evaluate

The answers could provide some surprises, and should set the church thinking about the effectiveness of its communications and the methods employed. The results could provoke the same kind of reflection as when, in chapter 3, local people were asked for their impressions of your church.

This is an important stage, as you need carefully to sift through a lot of opinions to look for widely-held viewpoints and key themes recurring in the responses. The results also need to be collated and presented in a format that can be easily understood by the church community. The findings should be communicated to them, either in a printed format, or preferably at a special presentation using an overhead projector so that each slide can be talked through and explained.

Determine action

Once the results have been made known and discussed at the relevant church committee or meeting, an action plan needs to be drawn up. This will spell out the steps to be taken as a result of the survey, and – very importantly – indicate who will be taking those steps.

The responsibility for introducing the changes could be given to one person, or to a small group of people, with a request to take action within a set period of time, say three months. If you do not have one already, this could be a good time to appoint a Communications Officer, responsible for co-ordinating all activities in this area (see Appendix I for an outline job description).

Build into the programme a timetable for taking a fresh look at your communications in perhaps a year or eighteen months' time. By then, everyone should be able to see the changes, and the improvements that have resulted – and probably think up some more!

Here is a survey of the main communication methods – printed, spoken and visual.

The printed word

Mind your language!

'Keep it simple!' is the best advice for anyone producing written material for use within the church or to communicate outside. The temptation to slip into jargon, abbreviations and 'in-words' is particularly strong when writing for the church family. After all, we all know what the YPF, BB, CMS and LDOS are . . . or do we?

As with news releases (see chapter 5) keep to short sentences, with your language as straightforward as possible. Your church probably includes people with a range of reading abilities. Remember also that not everyone has perfect vision, so take care when choosing the size of type or colour combinations which do not offer a good contrast between lettering and its background. Faint, washed-out type can render an otherwise well-produced leaflet unreadable for people with failing sight.

Try, in all situations, to put yourself in the place of the people with whom you are communicating, and ask yourself, 'Will they understand what I mean?' and 'What will make them read this?' Take every opportunity to check if people have read and understood what you meant. There is a saying which reads: 'I know you believe you understand what you think I said, but I'm not sure you realize that what you heard is not what I meant. . .' Don't let that be you!

Church magazines

'But we've always had one!' is the likely response to anyone brave enough to suggest that their church takes a close look at the magazine's role. It is an understandable response, particularly when the publication has been at the centre of church life for decades. Nevertheless, from time to time, it is worth asking 'why are we producing this?' Without a clear answer, the magazine can easily drift into serving no real purpose.

The range of contents of a typical church magazine could include:

- message from the church leadership,
- news of people and church groups,
- reports of church council or members' meetings,
- coming events,
- forthcoming activities of church organizations,
- prayer topics and Bible study material,
- house groups information,
- special section for children and young people,
- puzzles and crosswords on a Bible theme,
- news of the wider church, locally, nationally and internationally, including syndicated material supplied ready for printing.

All of these suggested contents promote the key themes of church communication outlined in chapter 7. The children's material brings teaching and encourages their involvement; the quizzes also educate. The editor's skill lies in choosing from this list, and balancing the contents so that as many readers as possible find the magazine interesting and attractive.

Many church magazines are also distributed to people on the 'fringe' of the church, such as those who attend only midweek activities, and it plays a part in encouraging increased involvement in church life. So the magazine has to look presentable – without absorbing so much time and energy that it takes on a life of its own, standing apart from the church.

In recent years, the monthly church magazine has lost much of its position as the main form of printed communication, as increasing numbers of churches now produce weekly noticesheets giving information on Sunday services and other activities in the coming week. In these churches, the magazine – where one still exists – tends to focus more on longer articles and reports of activities. Publication is often bi-monthly or every quarter. (Church newsletters for external distribution are discussed in chapter 4.)

Action

- What do you see as your magazine's objective and its main audience? How far is any secondary audience (e.g. friends of church members) taken into account?
- How far does your magazine contribute to the five key themes of church communication, outlined in chapter 7? Are any subjects covered which could not be placed under one of these headings?
- Is the magazine absorbing so much time in its production that it is becoming a major chore for the people involved? Would a change of format or frequency of publication avoid this and possibly improve the flow of information?
- When did you last carry out a readership survey? Devise a simple form listing the contents of the magazine, and ask readers to say which they found most useful or interesting. Allow replies to be anonymous!

Noticesheets

Weekly noticesheets or 'pewslips' give information on that Sunday's services and other activities, and usually also include details of forthcoming events. The format is usually a simple A4 or A5 sheet, photocopied on one or two sides. Often a pre-printed heading is used to give a better standard of presentation. One noticesheet editor described its role as acting as a 'friend in the know'. By reading it, newcomers would know exactly what was happening in the service and the activities coming up the following week.

A church covered by Administry's 1991 survey of church communications produced a guidance sheet outlining the type of material which could be included in the 'pewslip'. These contents are typical of many similar publications:

> *The pewslip is published weekly and covers:*
>
> > *a) the order of Sunday services.*
> > *b) the prayer diary for the following week.*
> > *c) 'official' church notices.*
>
> *Subject to space limitations, the pewslip also carries:*
>
> > *d) items submitted by the church council or pastoral leadership group (and their respective committees).*
> > *e) book reviews from our bookstall staff.*
> > *f) news and publicity for events which are open to all.*
> > *g) other information of specific help and/or interest to the congregation at large.*
>
> *For group activities which are of interest only to members, direct communication by mail or phone is recommended.*

Other churches also use the weekly noticesheet for brief items of family news or a message from the vicar or minister, perhaps supporting the sermon theme; or include summary information about events or activities with the name of someone to contact to find out more. The main challenge is knowing what to leave out so that the sheet remains useful as a brief communicator of vital information.

Action

If your church produces a weekly noticesheet:

- Is it welcoming to newcomers, explaining what is happening in church that day? Or is a level of knowledge about the church assumed?
- Is the noticesheet cluttered with information which could be communicated in other ways?
- Do you have a policy for setting out what items can be included?

If your church doesn't produce a noticesheet:

- How does it communicate the types of basic information that other churches publish in their noticesheets?
- Producing a weekly topical noticesheet can be time consuming, but would it allow you to reduce the length of the spoken announcements and/or the number of editions of the church magazine produced each year?

Letters

A letter from the church leadership to its members, each personally addressed and signed, can have impact – especially if it only occurs when important information needs to be communicated. A personal letter is more effective than a general appeal in the magazine, a notice on the board or a mention in the morning announcements. It is addressed to *you*, by name.

Modern word processing software packages make personalizing letters straightforward. Yet to ensure a genuine personal 'feel', each letter should be hand-addressed (Dear Charles. . .) and signed.

Churches using personal letters largely do so for financial appeals, where the needs of the church can be clearly set out, and each member of the church community is asked to make a specific response. The risk is when the church uses this method too often. The reaction changes from 'the pastor/vicar has written to me – it must be important' to 'Not another letter. . .'

The letters need not be posted, of course. They can be given out in church. You may like to consider whether the extra impact of the missive arriving direct on the doormat midweek outweighs the chance of being able to say a few explanatory words as you pass out the letters.

Action

- When was the last time the church leadership wrote to all the church members, and why?
- In what situation would a personal letter be the best way to communicate? Are there situations in your church where it would be useful for a letter to be adapted so that it was relevant to each member?

Financial information

One of the hardest subjects to communicate well is financial information. Few people have a grasp of those long lines of figures which, peculiarly, always seem to add up to identical totals at the bottom of the page!

The use of graphic designs can help understanding, and a wide range of software packages are available to transform the financial figures into pie or bar charts. Yet sometimes these also need explaining, and many people are more comfortable with explanations that they can relate directly to their own experience. Such as 'for every £1 which goes into the collection, 30p is spent on heating and lighting. . .'

Some churches have been especially inventive, as Administry discovered in a survey. Ideas unearthed included:

Cartoon by Micki Hounslow from Administry Resource Paper, *Called to Account*. © Administry. Reproduced with permission.

- arranging presentations styled on the TV game show, *The Price is Right*, with the congregation asked to guess how much was spent on key areas.
- transforming the church into a giant bar graph, with each pew representing a sum of money. People were then sent to set points along the aisle to act as markers, with those chosen having some link with the category. For example, under 'staff', the Rector; under 'buildings', a churchwarden.
- producing a brightly-iced cake to illustrate spending totals, and giving out slices of it to people in the meeting directly concerned with spending the money. As the cake was distributed, an explanation was given of how the money was spent.

Action

- Are you assuming that everyone understands your accounts? How could you make your financial information 'live' in people's minds?
- Consider the ideas above, and study how the popular newspapers and TV report the Budget or other major financial news.

Directories, prayer and programme cards

Directories giving the names, addresses and telephone numbers of the church officers and other members of the church family could be produced each year, at the time of the church's annual meeting. Some may also include their children's names. In some churches, the directory of members is combined with a prayer diary, so that members' names are grouped together for prayer on a particular day. In others, the list is included as part of the church's annual reports.

Prayer cards or bookmarks can be produced to remind church members to pray for a particular project or concern. Brief details of the topic are included along with points to pray about. Common examples are special outreach projects or missionaries.

Programme cards give information about activities organized by the church or church groups for the coming, say, three months. Contact numbers for more information are usually included. These cards are also useful as invitations to new members.

There is a range of professionally produced folders and cards which can be used for the prayer and programme cards, and these can dramatically improve their appearance. (See chapter 11.)

Action

- Could your church directory be transformed into a prayer diary?
- Does all your internal printed material conform with the church's design style and carry the church's logo?

Widening the vision. . .

How well informed is your church about what is happening in the wider Christian world – in your town, your diocese or area, the country and internationally? How can you help your church broaden their view of their part in a national or international ministry?

- *Magazine and newspaper racks.* Encourage members to subscribe to religious publications and to circulate them to others in the church. Have a rack where copies can be left for people to browse through or take home. (But make sure you have a regular sort-out so that piles of ancient copies don't become a fire hazard!) Publications from Christian societies and charities could also be circulated.
- *Newsletters from other churches.* Offer to swap your magazine for those produced by other local churches. Extracts from articles could be included in your own magazine, with the original copies left out to be read.
- *Bookstall.* Books to borrow or buy play a vital role in keeping any church family in touch with the world outside their walls, as well as helping their spiritual development. Bible reading notes are widely available in most churches.
- *Special services and events.* These give opportunities to focus on the needs of the wider world, and the work of Christian groups at home and overseas.

Action

- How many members of your church see the denomination's newspaper or other Christian publications regularly? How far could church leaders encourage this more widely? Could copies be bought for circulation? Have 'church agent' schemes been investigated with the publications concerned?
- How far could increased book reading be encouraged in your church? Could regular 'review spots' in services, or written reviews in magazines or newsletters, increase reading? Would special displays of books on a theme, or a 'Book Sunday'-style event give your bookstall more prominence?

The spoken word

Public speaking

Having to speak in public is one of life's most nerve-racking experiences. Even professional actors or politicians admit to nerves before facing an audience and say this helps them put their best into a performance. Public speaking is at the centre of most church services, with teaching and information being communicated to the congregation by word of mouth. The challenge for the leadership is to ensure that this regular, week-by-week use of speech in church life is an effective means of communication.

True, the Holy Spirit can enliven the dullest sermon so that it cuts deep into the hearts and minds of the people listening. It is also true that the preaching of God's word is never in vain, and will have an effect on those open to receive it. But, there is much that someone speaking in public can do to help their audience receive and understand the messages he or she is seeking to communicate. Many excellent books have been written about public speaking, and some of these are listed in chapter 11. Yet here are some points for you to consider:

- *Know your audience.* As with all forms of communication, you need to know what will interest your audience and consider what will make your talk relevant to them, for example, using illustrations from their experience, just as Jesus did. A reference drawn from this week's news will have more impact than, say, a parallel with the life of a nineteenth century poet.... Words or phrases not easily understood can place unnecessary barriers to listening. As you speak, maintain eye contact with your audience and watch when their attention starts to drift, so that you can change your pace or tone of voice, or use a helpful illustration to win back their interest.
- *Structure your message.* Imagine someone going home after hearing your talk and being asked, 'What did he/she speak about?' Try and identify in a sentence or two what you would like them to remember, then tailor your talk to make that your key point.

Deliver your talk in a logical sequence – there is a lot to be said for a 'three-point sermon', if everyone knows when each point begins and ends, and can remember them afterwards. Say when you have finished one section of your talk and are moving on to another. Briefly outline your subject at the outset and finish with a summary reinforcing the key points.
- *Help your audience.* People remember words when they are reinforced with pictures, so consider using relevant visual aids. The key word here is 'relevant'. If you take along a picture, or an overhead projector slide, that does not directly reinforce what you are saying, the audience will probably remember what you showed them ... without knowing *why* you showed it.

Use a flipchart or an overhead projector to add 'the signposts' along the route through your talk. They can emphasise key points, and give the audience a sense of progress. The temptation is trying to include every sentence of the talk, and so ending up with cluttered visual aids full of words which mask your main message.

Action

- What visual aid facilities are available in your church to help your speakers?
- Are your speakers – including your most experienced ones – encouraged to have training in public speaking, available from a range of church groups? Could you organize some within the church, perhaps using a video camera so the speakers can see themselves in action?

Church announcements

What is the reaction in your church when the time for 'the notices' arrives? Joyful anticipation? Time for a break from the worship? A chance to check your change for the collection?

Love them or loathe them, announcements form part of the vast majority of church services. Approaches to them vary widely. Some churches have them at the beginning of services, so they are separated from the worship and cover the period when some members of the congregation are still finding their seats. Others have them in the middle, so they can be the focus of prayers and integrated into the flow of the service. And sometimes notices come at the end, to separate them from the worship, and to ensure the congregation remembers key points as they leave.

The decision when to give the notices will be influenced by the 'comings and goings' of the congregation. Many churches, for example, time their announcements for when the Sunday school teachers are in the service so that they can be kept in touch with important news. The disadvantage, of course, is that the children are there as well, which can be distracting for people trying to hear what is being said. It is a balance which every church has to work out for itself.

Notices during the service get a higher level of attention from the congregation if they are delivered in a clear, interesting way, perhaps using visual aids. Church secretaries or vicars who use the same script every week are likely to soon lose their 'audience'. Listen carefully, and you can hear the youth group joining in...

Many churches have a policy of keeping the spoken announcements to activities of widespread interest. A member of one administration team told me: 'Because of the size of the church and the number of ministries, announcements from the pulpit are very selective and generally target large numbers of people.

'We use both the weekend and midweek printed service bulletins to announce events or needs, and individual ministries send out mailings to people involved in their area.'

Action

■ Are you announcing information that is already being communicated elsewhere? If the church has a weekly noticesheet, is there any point in repeating all the information? Consider keeping the spoken notices to stress important items affecting large numbers of the church family.

■ Are your notices presented in the same way each week? Why not have a rota of people giving the notices, so that the style of presentation is different. Is there any scope for using the overhead projector or other visual aids?

■ How about developing the notices? Some churches combine 'the announcements' with a 'family time' when a special welcome is given to anyone who has a birthday or is returning after sickness or service elsewhere. Members of the congregation are invited to share any import-

ant news. The notices play an important part in developing the family 'feel' of the church.
■ Are you providing brief announcements for use at midweek groups and activities? Would this reduce the Sunday announcements?

Church business meetings

The format of church meetings varies considerably depending on the denomination and the amount of authority vested in them. In some churches, the meetings are held to gain viewpoints which will be taken into consideration when decisions are made; in other churches, the meeting makes the decision.

Business meetings differ from many other forms of communication reviewed above, because they are aimed at obtaining feedback and opinions. A sign of a successful meeting is that everyone feels they have understood the subjects under discussion and have had the opportunity of expressing their viewpoint, preferably before midnight! So how to achieve this?

■ *Know why you are holding the meeting.* What do you want to achieve by the end of the meeting? Be as specific as possible, so that you know whether you have been successful. Examples could be 'to gain support for the new building project' or 'to obtain four realistic proposals for local outreach', with an agreed plan of action.
■ *Know what you want to discuss, and the decisions you are seeing.* This comes down to having an agenda which ensures that all the key items of business can be covered. Not all the items on the agenda will be as important, so the person chairing the meeting should decide in advance roughly how much time should be devoted to each item.
■ *Make sure everyone has enough information to make an informed decision, including issuing papers in advance.* We

all like to understand what it is we are being asked to support or comment upon. For more complex issues, time can be saved by issuing information in advance and asking people to read it before they come. Then, at the meeting, a brief summary can be given and questions invited.

- *Make sure people have enough opportunity to make their views known.* Easier said than done. In most groups, there are people who are more willing than others to give their opinions. A good chairperson encourages everyone to have their say, without leaving long, lingering silences that hang heavy and stifle the flow of the meeting.
- *Keep good records, so that you know what you have decided and can move forward from that point.* It could be the agreement or rejection of a proposal put to the meeting; or a decision to obtain more information, and to discuss the subject again at a later meeting (and you need to know exactly what information and which 'later meeting'!); or it could be some wording which sums up the range of views expressed at the meeting, so the subject can be examined elsewhere (perhaps in a smaller group) in more detail, and proposals brought back to the church at a specified later meeting.

Action

- How special is your annual church meeting? Is it just a chance to re-elect the officers? Or could it be used for a major presentation or discussion of strategy for the year ahead. Is there scope in your church to organize a 'not-to-be-missed' session on 'The Way Ahead'?
- Which of your recent business meetings have been the best attended? What was on the agenda? Was it something which directly affected everyone? Are there lessons to be learnt from this about the content of meetings?
- At what time do you hold your meetings? Are refreshments provided? Does the layout of the chairs encourage

discussion? Do you sometimes break into smaller groups to enable more people to speak and express a viewpoint? (The groups could then report back to the meeting on their discussions).

- Could the 'business' part of the meeting be linked to a time of worship, prayer or teaching so that it is not divorced from other parts of church life?

The grapevine

Every organization, large and small, has 'a grapevine'. This is the informal way that information travels from person to person, on the lines of 'Guess what I just heard!' The grapevine tends to move the information quickly, but seldom with total accuracy. The longer the chain from the person first communicating the information to the last one receiving it, the more likely is the message to be 'transformed'.

The challenge is to keep lines of communications short, so that as many people as possible receive the message first-hand, either by word of mouth or on paper. Many churches use church council or diaconate members to communicate information, to short-cut the grapevine.

Action

- Do you have examples of information being distorted as it has passed from person to person within the church? Would the use of a 'briefing system', with identified people being responsible for communicating a message, work in your church?

The telephone

Where would we be without the telephone? Is it possible to go anywhere these days and not find someone using a mobile phone? The telephone has become a taken-for-granted piece of equipment linking every part of our lives. Does it have a role as part of a church's network of communications?

Action

■ How quickly can news be passed around your church when urgent prayer or other action is needed? Do you have a 'prayer link' set up, so that a need can be communicated fast through a pre-arranged network of people.

■ Some churches have a pre-recorded tape which gives information on church activities by telephone. Callers needing more details can contact the main church number. Would this be worthwhile in your church?

■ How welcoming is your church answerphone? Does it encourage people to leave a message, or suggest a specific time when the phone will be answered by a real person?

Audio tapes

Cassette tapes have long been keeping church members in touch. Services and meetings are routinely recorded for the benefit of those unable to attend. Missionaries, and members of the church family away from home, send back tapes to keep the church informed of their activities. Bible study and teaching tapes are in common use for group and individual use. Is there scope for extending their use?

Action

■ Produce a brief bulletin of church news and prayer topics, no more than five minutes, which could be given to house groups for them to use. This ensures the same information is given at each meeting.

■ Record a series of brief interviews reflecting the range of views held on a subject, then play this to set the scene before further discussion at a church meeting.

Visual communications

Noticeboards and displays

'We use noticeboards for displaying things we don't want people to see!' one church told Administry's communications survey. It is an understandable viewpoint, particularly when many noticeboards look like gardens in need of a good weeding. Notices and posters of all shapes and sizes just keep appearing . . . and stay there until they fall off with age.

Many people ignore noticeboards. There are just too many other things to do after the service. There are people to speak to and catch up on their news and so little time to study the notices on the board. But noticeboards *do* have a role to play.

- They remind people about information that has been communicated to them by other means, for example a reminder of a special event announced in church or included in the noticesheet or magazine.
- They communicate specific information about a group's activities to members of that group who know where the information will be displayed, for example the duty rota of stewards.
- They convey visual information, such as photos of church officers, members or recent events.

One London parish church, blessed with a long passageway, erected a series of noticeboards on either side. Each is devoted to photographs, posters and information about a specific church activity. Most churches are not as fortunate!

Displays are usually produced for a specific purpose, perhaps to give information on a charity the church is supporting, or to mark an anniversary or another event, or maybe to introduce the church itself. By their nature, displays are specially produced and seek to attract atten-

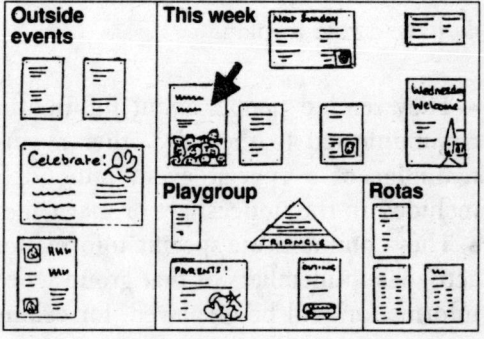

Which is yours?
© Administry. Reproduced with permission.

tion for a fixed period of time (unlike noticeboards, which are permanent). Displays need to be able to attract attention at a glance and encourage people to study its information. A combination of large eye-catching material, such as posters or pictures, could be used with more wordy material for people who want to read more information – all supported by some take-away leaflets.

Action

- Carry out a survey of your noticeboards. Do you have enough of them? Are they in places where they can be seen, without causing a bottle-neck in a busy passage? If you have a side-door used by visitors during the week, is there a noticeboard facing the entrance?
- Do you have a policy to decide what goes up on the noticeboards? Is there, for example, a board available to local groups who use your building?
- Is someone responsible for making sure each noticeboard stays looking good and up-to-date?
- Could the boards be divided into areas of interest, with space for the youth group, Sunday school, missionary activities, etc.?
- Is there scope for your church to design a permanent display, introducing itself and its activities, which could be left where visitors can see it. Church members would, of course, be on hand to answer questions and give a warm welcome!

Video

The age of the home video recorder and portable camcorder has arrived in increasing numbers of homes, and video cameras have come to church to do more than just record the weddings. Video has an important communications role. Some applications include:

- introducing the church on a videotape which could be played at church open days, or loaned to people considering joining the church.
- keeping in touch with church workers serving overseas, or with former members of the church who have moved away.
- education and evangelism, using the range of well-produced materials available.
- recording services to pass on to members of the church

unable to attend.
- making a video as a teamwork project for a church group, for example the youth group producing a video on the needs of the local area.
- using videos produced by Christian organizations to keep your church in touch with the wider world.
- illustrating reports for church business meetings.

Take action

Now is the time to move forward with your communications audit. Take another look through this chapter and make notes of any ideas which come to you as you read. List all your types of internal church communication and begin to think through how effectively each is working. Use the 'D.A.R.E.D.' approach at the beginning of this chapter to plan how to implement your audit, and be prepared to make some changes to the way you communicate.

CHAPTER NINE
Putting it all together

Now we can bring together the full range of communications, both inside the church, and from the church to the world outside. Three typical publicity projects offer the chance to combine a range of communications. They are:
- Announcing a new church leader,
- Launching a parent and toddler group,
- Publicizing a town-wide outreach campaign.

Each of the projects is set out in a similar format based on three stages:

- *Research* – making sure you have as much information as possible before you spring into action.
- *Audience* – identifying precisely those people with whom you want to communicate, so that all your efforts can be closely targeted.
- *Strategy* – using your research, and knowledge of your audience, to launch your campaign.

Work through the examples set out below. Before reading each section, consider what research you would carry out, which target audiences you would identify, and the strategy you would adopt. Try not to read through a section until you have planned your course of action. Then compare it with the suggestions in each case study.

A new church leader

The choice had finally been made. Blanktown Evangelical's new minister had been appointed and would arrive in about ten weeks' time. The date for his induction service had been set and Roy, the communications officer, had been asked to come up with some ideas to publicize his arrival, and to use this as a way of raising awareness of the church in the area.

Research

Before drawing up plans and ideas, Roy set out to find out as much as he could about the new minister and his family. He already knew a lot about him because of the church's selection process. The man had preached at the church and had met with church members afterwards. But Roy wanted to make sure he had as full a picture as possible. So he asked the church secretary for his telephone number, and before calling jotted down a list of questions.

Where was he serving now, and where had he worked previously, and trained?
What was his present church like? Did he expect many differences in his new church?
Did he already have any links with his new area?
What did he do before joining the ministry?
Where did he grow up, go to school etc?
Is he married, wife's name etc. Details of any children.
Is he involved with any church interest groups, such as missionary societies?
What were his interests/hobbies outside the church?
How old is he?
Did he have a 'message' he would like to send as a greeting to the people in the area?

When Roy spoke to the new minister, he found that many of his questions led naturally to others as the conversation developed, and he soon felt that he had a good impression of the man who was coming to the church.

Audience

Now that Roy had this information, he jotted down the audiences to which it should be communicated.

- *Members of the church congregation.*
- *Those who attended church-related activities, such as the 'drop-in'.*
- *People living in the area.*
- *The wider denomination.*
- *Leaders of other local churches.*
- *People active locally in the areas where the new minister showed particular interest, e.g. third world issues or homelessness.*

Strategy

Timing

Most information would be released during the two weeks before the new minister's induction service.

Action

- Write a news release on the new minister, and issue it to newspapers in good time for them to take their own photographs and publish these in the edition closest to the induction. (If the minister has a particular interest, or is widely known, produce a version for the denominational newspapers.)
- Have some photographs taken of the minister for use with the local media and in other publications.
- Speak to the editor about the possibility of the minister

writing one of the newspaper's weekly comment columns, perhaps describing his first impressions of his new area.
- Contact the local radio stations' religious and news programmes, and offer them an interview with the minister. Since the stations cover wide areas, Roy tried to think up a news story likely to attract their interest – a new minister was not enough of a story of itself. (How about the minister's concern for the homeless, and his assessment of local needs?)
- Write an article for the church magazine, longer than the news release with more information, using an interview-style format to bring out more about the minister's personality and ideas for the church.
- Produce a leaflet introducing the new minister and inviting local people to attend the induction service. Include general information on the church and details of how to contact the minister.
- Write a letter to all local churches, introducing the minister and inviting them to send representatives to the induction service. Consider inviting the local mayor, MP and councillors.
- Put up a poster outside the church welcoming the minister, and mount a display at the induction service introducing the church.
- Change local databases at information centres and libraries.

All the above actions would be co-ordinated with 'welcome events' being arranged at the church. Most importantly, they would also need to be co-ordinated and agreed with the minister himself who should be fully involved in the planning.

Parent-and-toddler group

> *Joan Sidmouth approached publicity officer Jenny Dalton after the morning service at St Mary's Church. 'Have you heard about the plan to start a*

parents-and-toddlers group? It's due to be up and running after Easter. Can you help?'

Research

Jenny agreed to meet with Joan on Thursday evening, and in the meantime thought about the sort of information she would need.

- When and where is the club to be held?
- For what ages of children?
- What facilities will be available to them?
- Will there be any charge?
- Why were they starting the club?
- Was there a need for one locally?
- How many volunteers would be staffing it?

Audience

When Jenny and Joan met, they ran through the questions and sought to identify the different groups who should know about the club:

- parents with young children living locally,
- professionals working with families locally, e.g. health visitors, social workers, childminders,
- members of the church community, as a source of helpers and prayer support,
- local centres of information, such as libraries, information bureaux and Citizens Advice Bureaux.

Joan stressed that their own research, talking to young mums, etc., had indicated that there was a great need for the club, and that little effort would be needed to attract parents to use it. The difficulty would be to keep numbers down to a manageable level. The church premises were small and they did not want to build up a long waiting list.

Strategy

Publicity within the church to begin about 4–6 weeks before the group opened. Other publicity 2–3 weeks before the opening.

Action

Given the need to avoid attracting too much response, the best form of publicity would be low-key, by word of mouth from young parents in the church to their non-church friends. If this did not attract enough interest, other forms of low-key publicity could be used, including posters in local shops and outside the church.

The setting up of the group was announced in church, and requests for help with running it were placed in several editions of the church's weekly noticesheet before the opening. A poster giving details was prominently displayed inside the church foyer. Jenny designed an attractive leaflet that set out all the details of the club to be handed out as a reminder by the church mums when telling their friends. Copies of the leaflet were given to the local health centre for the staff's information, and for the noticeboard. Copies also went to the local social services office so that staff there could refer parents.

Jenny kept in touch with the group organizers. As expected, the group was a success and needed little extra publicity. When numbers began to drop off, the leaflet was revised and distributed. Regular updates about the group were included in the monthly church magazine.

At one stage, Jenny and Joan considered placing a poster outside the church advertising the group, and inviting the local papers to come and take photographs of the group's annual party. Although both would have been good publicity for the group, they agreed that this could have resulted in people coming to join the club, and being turned away. This could have resulted in some ill-feeling locally. The project, to date, had been an example of publicity being used selectively to achieve a specific goal. Joan was working on plans to set up a second group, meeting on a different day of the week...

City-wide mission

Joe Andrews, pentecostal pastor and chairman of the organizers of 'Message 2000' the town-wide outreach campaign planned for Blanktown, was a worried man. There were just eight months left until the opening of the ten-day event, and much of the planning still had to be done. He gathered together a cross-section of local church leaders who formed a co-ordinating committee, and asked them for their ideas on publicity.

'We've got someone who can design posters,' said one minister. 'Our magazine editor is very keen,' said another. 'My curate writes well,' volunteered the vicar of the town's largest Anglican church. 'Our publicity secretary would love to help,' announced Pastor Jenkins, taking Frank Jeffrey's support as an act of faith.

This, decided Joe Andrews, was what he needed: a person who could co-ordinate all the publicity aspects of the event, leaving him and the other church leaders free to oversee the spiritual dimension. Frank Jeffrey could put together a small team, using the specialist volunteers from the other churches...

Research

Frank met Joe in the front room of his home near the church, and sought to find out as much as he could about the event. He had heard of it, briefly, from his own pastor who had made reference to it in a sermon a month or so before. He asked Joe Andrews for the following details:

- *the dates and venues for the event.*

- how many people these venues could hold.
- the details of the people taking part. Were there any well-known names, locally or from further afield?
- the types of activities taking place.
- the details of the churches supporting the event.
- how would it be financed?
- were there special events for different groups, e.g. children or young people?
- why was the event being organized at this time?
- would there be any special emphasis, e.g. healing.

And, importantly,

- how much would there be to spend on publicity?
- who would approve this spending, and the format of the publicity?

Audience

Put simply, there were three main audiences.

1 Christian believers in the town's churches. It would be essential to ensure that they had as much information about the event as possible, were fully committed to support it, and would encourage their non-church friends and neighbours to attend.
2 Local people with some contact with their local church, perhaps by attending a mid-week activity, although not committed to the church.
3 Local people not involved in the town's churches. They would form the main evangelistic 'target' of the event, and could be further divided into age groups, where they lived, etc.

Strategy

More than either of the previous two examples, planning and timing are of major importance here. Activities must be co-ordinated from at least six months before, with the intention of building to a publicity 'peak' just before the opening of the event. In outline the programme could run like this:

Six months before the event, raise awareness of 'Message 2000' in all the town's churches by:
- producing material for church magazines.
- launching a newsletter for distribution in the churches.
- producing posters and leaflets for use in churches.
- producing visual aids, displays and a short video for showing at meetings in the local churches (to let church leaders use the material themselves, and demonstrate their support).

All these materials would carry a clearly identifiable 'logo' for the event, which would appear on all publicity initiatied by the event organizers.

Issue a news release saying that the event has been organized, but without giving too many details. This would be to let the wider public begin to hear of the event, as well as to inform churchgoers whose ministers were not, as yet, publicizing it.

Awareness-raising activities could continue during the following five months, with regular information being issued to the churches. Then. . .

Six weeks before, contact the AA or RAC to have sign-posting put up to direct people to the major venues during the event.

One month before, the tempo is raised with advertisements appearing in the local press and on posterboards around the town. The aim here is to raise interest and awareness on the part of non-churchgoing local people.

Detailed information on the event is made available to local churches for them to begin publicizing it to people with whom they are in direct contact.

Two weeks before, the campaign is reinforced by local radio advertising and full information issued to the media about the event. Photographs are taken to give to the local press. Eye-catching display material is distributed to all supporting churches for them to use outside their buildings to demonstrate their support and involvement, and complement the paid advertising.

The publicity has moved from arousing interest to winning full attention for the event. This is when associated outdoor events, such as street theatre and information stalls in the town centre, would be used, with the momentum maintained until the event is in full swing. A local, short-term radio station could be established, which would broadcast for twenty-eight days (see chapter 10).

Now is the time, too, for local church members to show their support by reinforcing the advertising with car stickers and house posters displaying the logo. All types of publicity should reinforce each other at this stage, including leaflets and brochures delivered house to house during this period.

When the event finally happens, the publicity momentum needs to be kept up, with local journalists being encouraged to visit the venues, and churches being encouraged to create their own publicity activities. As far as possible, take the event out into the community, with 'satellite' events taking place in different parts of the town, each well-publicized.

Keep monitoring the feedback on the publicity. Ask people at the event how they heard about it. Conduct surveys to see how many people are aware of what is happening, and what level of knowledge they have.

When it is all over, see what lessons you can learn for the next time you have to publicize such a major event. Work on the basis that there will be a next time!

CHAPTER TEN
The way ahead

Standing in a converted Birmingham warehouse, I was fascinated by the teenager in front of me. Totally absorbed in his own world, he was fighting battles and finding his way through a castle labyrinth. His field of vision was displayed on the screen above our heads, and 'the sword' he was holding clearly depicted in computer graphics. This was the world of 'virtual reality', where players 'go within' a computer program to interact with figures and landscapes that exist only in the mind of the programmer and player.

It was eerie to see the teenager totally immersed in this virtual 'unreality', which was as real to him as I would have been had he taken off the player's mask. Just a short time ago, this would have been science fiction. Today, it is just one step beyond the computer games that have so many people addicted to their screens. As I watched him, I wondered if one day churches would be producing 'virtual reality' software. Their aim? To give people the experience of joining in a service without leaving their armchairs at home. A chilling glimpse, perhaps, of tomorrow.

The role of the prophet

A prophet, they say, is a person with the Bible in one hand and a newspaper in the other. They analyse today's events in the light of Scripture and catch sight of things to come.

Looking beyond tomorrow is never easy, especially in the fast-moving world of the media. Who, for example, would have forecast the popularity of so-called 'adult' comics like *Viz*? Or that black-and-white videos of *Watch with Mother* children's programmes would be best-sellers more than thirty years after their first broadcast. Or how satellite TV has transformed the face of the English football league? The challenge for Christian communicators lies in looking for new opportunities to project the gospel message, and more effective ways of keeping the church family in touch.

In recent years, the major success of innovative Radio Cracker and March For Jesus events has demonstrated new ways of taking the church out into the community. Local Radio Cracker stations were organized at Christmas in around one hundred UK centres in 1991 and 1992, with church youth groups raising money for Third World need, learning skills in radio, and communicating the real meaning of Christmas. March For Jesus has motivated many thousands of Christians around Britain – and now Europe and further afield – to march through their localities proclaiming the gospel message. Just a few years back, these would have been glimmers in someone's prayer life.

Changes in technology and government controls have presented major opportunities for communicating the Christian message. The Churches Advisory Council for Local Broadcasting is leading moves to encourage Christians to take advantage of the new openings. General secretary Jeff Bonser explains:

> *The Decade of Evangelism is also a decade of new opportunity in broadcasting. Independent radio will expand considerably in the 1990s. Multi-channel cable TV is expected to be available to most people this decade, and could include a locally-produced community channel.*

> There are also opportunities for religious ownership of local/community radio stations, cable TV and satellite channels, plus religious advertising and sponsorship.

Television

A hard-hitting promotional video made by Christian TV producers, CVG Television of Birmingham makes a telling point. Millions of viewers are tuned into TV every night of the week, while the Church still puts much of its resources into reaching people with the printed word.

CVG director Aden Murcott spells out the challenge of the TV age and challenges Christians to play their part in making use of the medium. He explains: 'With the power of television harnessed for good, we could be reaching behind millions of closed doors every day, returning lost values and reinstating Christian principles and practices into people's lives.'

CVG is one of a growing number of groups seeking to make use of increasing opportunities in the fast-changing world of TV and video. Vision Broadcasting, Britain's first Christian TV channel, began broadcasting programmes in 1986 and sees itself as 'the role model for Christian TV channels in the UK'. In late 1992, its programmes were being seen on thirteen cable stations. The programmes covered:

- children, family and local church involvement,
- current affairs and social issues from a Christian point of view,
- personal testimonies and devotional programmes.

Some of the organizations contributing video material for the output included the Salvation Army, the Missionary Aviation Fellowship, Coventry Cathedral and a local church in Bath. Vision Broadcasting gives Christians in the area where its programmes are being screened the opportunity to be involved in those programmes, and for their own videos to be considered for broadcast. The Swindon-based organization sees great potential in the fast-expanding availability of satellite and cable TV. It is dedicated to putting Christian programmes onto every cable station, and only accepts programmes and advertisements from organizations, churches and other bodies who 'identify with Christian ethics'. On the importance of gaining a role for Christianity in broadcasting, Vision's chief executive Fran Wildish explains: 'If a product is not on TV then it is deemed to have no value in our society.'

The American influence

While Vision Broadcasting is a home-grown initiative, Christian groups from the United States have been quick to spot the opportunities in the liberalization of the UK broadcasting scene. Supporters of evangelist Morris Cerullo are being encouraged to finance a twenty-four-hour Christian TV network to European satellite and cable viewers. In October 1992, Greg Mauro, European director of the Morris Cerullo organization, said they were in contact with a range of UK Christian groups to work together on British programmes for their output.

International Family Entertainment, the US-based organization led by evangelist Pat Robertson, has announced plans to bring his 'Family Channel', which reaches 54 million American homes, into Britain.

Some British churchgoers have expressed fears of an influx of American-style TV evangelists onto the UK Christian scene. The banning of on-air appeals for funds by broadcasters means, they say, that home-grown British stations would be at a major disadvantage, as the American evangelists could simply rely on donations from the US to finance their output.

The critics of the new regulations also point gloomily

to the demise of the Sunday evening 'God slot' on ITV and predict that the BBC will soon follow suit. It is little consolation to them that ITV will still have to carry at least two hours of religious broadcasting at some time during the week.

Some Christian groups have also expressed concern that direct evangelistic appeals to the camera are outlawed by the new codes. Defending the Independent Television Commission from its critics, religious broadcasting officer Rachel Viney wrote of the new programme codes: 'It's important to remember that the audience for most channels will include those of all faiths and those of none. Respect for the viewer, whatever his or her belief, therefore underpins the codes.'

TV Advertising

From 1993, religious advertising is now allowed on broadcast and satellite TV, and stations are able to accept ads that:

- publicize events, such as services, meetings or religious festivals,
- describe an organization's activities and how to contact it,
- offer publications or promote the sale or rental of other merchandise.

Advertising that 'expounds religious doctrine' is not acceptable.

The Church of England is among Christian groups considering how they could make use of these new opportunities. The Diocese of Lichfield made some pilot TV commercials which were screened in the Midlands in January 1993. One option could be to launch a TV campaign and encourage churches to support it with local posters, leaflets and events. Such an initiative could be launched at Christmas or Easter to boost churchgoing numbers.

Critics have said that TV advertising is a poor medium by which to communicate a message about faith, and its costs are likely to deter all but the wealthiest organizations. These, they argue, are unlikely to be British...

Radio

Madonna, Elvis Presley, Cher, politicians, sportsmen and comedians all featured in a BBC poster campaign during 1992. It extolled the benefits of BBC radio, with the slogan 'It's all for you on Radio Two'. Happy listeners were shown gardening or fishing while all these stars competed for their attention.

Hidden away, between the cartoons of pop stars living and dead, jockeys, musicians and footballers, was a bishop battling to make his point against the frantic activity all around him. It was a reference to Radio Two's *Pause for Thought* slots and its other religious output. The posters illustrated for me the church's challenge to make the best use of opportunities in radio. There could be many more openings in coming years.

During the 1990s, up to 300 more community radio stations could be licensed. The opportunity to own a station is available to virtually anyone, with the Radio Authority choosing the successful candidate from groups that apply. In some areas, Christians have joined with others in the community to bid for the licences, which run for eight years.

Wear FM, launched in November 1990, covers a potential audience of more than 250,000 in Sunderland and beyond. The churches were involved from the outset, and the station's chairman, Canon Granville Gibson, is Rector of Sunderland and Rural Dean of Wearmouth. The station broadcasts twenty-four hours a day, seven days a week, with a range of programmes which reflect the interests of the community. Religious broadcasting, involving all faiths represented in the area, forms part of its programming.

In High Wycombe, members of several local churches joined together to launch an application. They stressed that, if successful, the station would be 'for the community', and not just for the churches. In January 1993, Radio Wye heard that its application had been successful, and it is due to be on air by the end of the year.

Tips on how to approach local station managers of new and existing stations are given by Edwin Robertson in *Air Your Faith* (Jay Books), a guide to the growing opportunities for Christians in radio. He advises:

> *Religion is notoriously marginal and the station manager will need persuading that that is what his listeners want. We may want to air our faith, but who wants to listen?*
>
> *As well as persuading him that within the churches there are people who care about the community and possibly some of his advertisers, we need to influence him in his priorities of what is good for the community. Christians who want to air their faith must be seen as allies in an effort to build up or preserve a healthy community life, which can be the life blood of a radio station.*

Community radio stations are likely to be especially interested in local churches who are willing to work alongside the station's staff to help reflect the life of the area. Churches who can supply volunteers to help with the station's running and provide contact with local grassroots activity are far more likely to gain a welcome than those who only want to broadcast evangelistic messages.

The support of a broad range of the area's churches, perhaps through the local 'Churches Together' group, will be welcomed by groups applying for licences who will be keen to build relationships with the community. The sooner churches become involved, the more likely they are to influence the station's programming.

Satellite TV viewers can now also pick up Christian radio channels! Since October 1992, United Christian Broadcasters have been using an audio channel linked to the Astra satellite to present a mix of Christian music and 'chat'. Ian Mackie, managing director of UCB, told me:

> *We are now in a position to share the gospel to millions of people throughout Western Europe by broadcasting Christian programming in a relevant and attractive way.*
>
> *Our research has confirmed that Christian music is a very powerful communications tool which comforts and encourages all who listen to our station. We also found that in this way we can attract a non-Christian audience who want to know more about the faith and yet we do not have to compromise the gospel message.*

Trans World Radio are also using the Astra satellite to broadcast a one-hour news and current affairs programme each morning 'on the back' of the Sky Movies channel.

The opportunity to tune in to radio stations via satellite is available to most BSkyB subscribers by pressing a button on the remote control when tuned to the appropriate TV channel. The satellite receiver's audio output can be linked directly to a hi-fi system so that the TV does not need to be switched on.

Special event or 'restricted licence' radio has also opened up new opportunities for Christian broadcasters. These twenty-eight-day licences covering a local area were first used by the Greenbelt Arts Festival, and provided the platform for the Radio Cracker project in 1991 and 1992. From Aberdeen to Amersham, from Belfast to Broadstairs, ninety FM Radio Cracker stations first took to the air in December 1991, closing down on Christmas Eve. They were staffed by mainly young people, raising money for Third World projects.

Christians taking part in some major March For Jesus events during 1992 were asked to bring personal stereos so they could tune into MFJ Radio, another use of a 'restricted licence'. Marchers were kept in touch with information and the music to march to.

Another example of a temporary licence being used in support of outreach occurred in October 1992, when a local radio station was set up at the end of Southend pier as part of 'The Big Event', a week-long outreach initiative, supported by more than a hundred Essex churches.

Plans have been unveiled to try to set up London Christian Radio, a Christian station broadcasting to 10 million people in the capital and beyond. Several licences were due to be advertised in March 1993, with competition for these likely to be fierce. Consultations involving around 700 church leaders were held across London and the Home Counties in November 1992. The vision presented was for a station broadcasting seven days a week, twenty-four hours a day, providing news and views, analysis and comment, teaching, advice and help. The station's supporters said: 'London Christian Radio will help ordinary Christians be more clear about their faith – and how it applies to daily living. It will help those outside the Church understand what it means to follow Jesus.'

The printed word

In 1992, magazine readers could choose from 2,400 different titles – up from 1,500 ten years earlier. New magazines tend to focus on a specialist area, such as users of a particular type of computer. So advertisers are guaranteed a closely-defined audience and readers who are deeply interested in the subject.

There are 1,265 local newspapers in the UK, with six million copies being circulated every weekday. Increasing numbers are 'freesheets', delivered without cost to the reader. More than half the adults in the UK read a national newspaper every day, but their combined circulations have dropped by nearly ten per cent over the past ten years.

The trend? People are still reading despite the sharp rise in TV and radio. Yet they seem increasingly to be reading publications of direct concern to them – magazines and newspapers which directly address their interests or the place where they live. The quality of the publications is fast improving, with colour photographs now appearing in even the most humble local freesheet.

The message for the Christian communicator in print is clear. To be read, our newsletters, brochures and leaflets will need to be increasingly well-produced and closely aimed at our audience. The new desktop publishing technologies and advances in printing will need to be used to the full.

Increasingly, a choice may have to be made between publishing a printed item and producing a video. How long before churches are routinely delivering the newsletter on video, door to door? Already testimonies on video are proving more acceptable to give to non-Christian friends than printed tracts.

At the outset of this book, I stressed that communicating is 'more than just words'. Communicating the Christian message takes more than words in print, on TV screens or on the airwaves. The best words in the world mean nothing unless they are supported by actions.

The future could find our communities increasingly fragmented. The dozens of TV channels and radio stations available in every town could mean no two houses in a street are tuned into the same programmes. In the same house, each family member could be tuned into something different with no communication between them. Computer systems will make electronic shopping from home commonplace, and increasing numbers of people will switch to tele-working from their homes. The need to 'go out' and meet other people could soon fall away...

The breaking down of the community could bring increasing challenges for the Church – including the role of helping to bring people together, not just to worship, but simply to meet others. Christian groups like the Shaftesbury Society are working hard in inner city areas, helping to revive community feeling and encourage people to communicate with their neighbours. Churches could have a growing role in helping local society stay alive.

Luncheon clubs, drop-in centres, parents' groups, youth activities, support for victims of crime, advice centres, playschemes and keep-fit sessions – they could all have an increasing part to play as the Church strives to earn its right to be heard. Shorter hours for those in work, earlier retirement and longer life expectancy will all play a role in shaping how we live in the late 1990s and beyond.

The church's vital role of communicating, in word and deed, may soon be essential to keep society alive ... for this world, and the next.

CHAPTER ELEVEN
Where to turn for help

Books to read

Titles to help church communications officers find out more about modern public relations practice:

Sam Black, *Introduction to Public Relations*, Modino.
Roger Haywood, *All About Public Relations*, McGraw Hill.
Wilfred Howard (ed.), *The Practice of Public Relations*, Heinemann.
Frank Jefkins, *Planned Press and Public Relations*, Pitman.
Frank Jefkins, *Public Relations*, Pitman.
Reginald Peplow, *The Good Publicity Guide*, Sheldon Press.
Michael Bland, *Be Your Own PR Man*, Kogan Page.
Patrick Quinn, *The Secrets of Successful Low-Budget Advertising*, Heinemann.
Alastair Crompton, *Do Your Own Advertising*, Business Books.
Bill Penn, *Be Your Own PR Expert*, Piatkus.
Ron Ludlow and Fergus Panton, *The Essence of Effective Communication*, Prentice Hall.

Many of these books should be available at your local library, under 'Management' section 659.

The author recommends...

There are many books on communication so I have tried to pick out those that I have found of most use in church-based communication.

A wide range of books on Christian communications, including video, magazines, bookstalls and radio are published by Jay Books, 30 The Boundary, Langton Green, Tunbridge Wells, Kent TN3 0YB. These include: Kim Cook, *Communicate! A Guide to Basic PR for Christians.*

Palm Tree Press, Rattlesden, Bury St Edmunds, Suffolk IP30 0SZ produce an excellent range of copyright free 'instant art' books for use in church publications, as well as two practical guides to help church communicators: *How to Produce a Church Magazine*, by John Cole – particularly useful sections on page layout and writing style; and *How to be a Local Church*, also by John Cole.

Mike Purdie, *The Complete Desktop Publisher*, Purdie Publishing, PO Box 129, Staines, Middlessex TW18 3PL. An easy-to-follow guide to assist churches producing magazines, newsletters and other materials by means of desktop publishing. It includes a valuable section on design.

Running meetings

Milo O Frank, *How to run a successful meeting in half the time*, Corgi Books.
Marion E Haynes, *Effective Meeting Skills*, Kogan Page.

Public speaking

John Campbell, *Speak for Yourself*, BBC Books.
Dale Carnegie, *How to Develop Self Confidence and Influence People by Public Speaking*, Cedar.
Greville Janner, *Janner on Communication*, Hutchinson Business Books – practical advice on public speaking as well as other forms of communication.

Frederick Crix, *Taking a Lead*, Scripture Union – very readable sections on preaching and leading worship.

Video communications

Andrew Crofts, *Using Television & Video in Business*, Mercury.
Mandy Matson, *Using Your Camcorder*, Amphoto.
Malcolm Squires, *The Camcorder Handbook*, Headline.

Drama

Alan MacDonald, Steve Stickley and Philip Hawthorn, *Street Theatre*, Minstrel/Monarch Publications.
Alan MacDonald and Steve Stickley, *The Drama Recipe Book*, Minstrel/Monarch Publications.
Paul Burbridge and Murray Watts, *Time to Act*, Hodder & Stoughton.

Broadcasting

Edwin Robertson, *Air Your Faith*, Jay Books.
Grace Baptist Mission, *A Layman's Guide to 'Topical Thoughts'*, 12 Abbey Close, Abingdon OX14 3JD.
Charles Handy, *Waiting for the Mountain to Move*, Hutchinson – a collection of the author's 'Thoughts for the Day'.
Rosemary Horstmann, *Writing for Radio*, A & C Black – one of a series of books on writing for different markets.
Peter Tidman and H Lloyd Slater, *Tidman's Media Interview Technique*, Kogan Page.
Michael Bland and Simone Mondesir, *Promoting Yourself on Television and Radio*, Kogan Page.

Church strategy (including communications)

John Finney, *The Well-Church Book*, Scripture Union.
David Cohen and Stephen Gaukroger, *How to Close Your Church in a Decade*, Scripture Union.

Eddie Gibbs, *I Believe in Church Growth*, Hodder & Stoughton.
David Watson, *I Believe in Evangelism*, Hodder & Stoughton.
Fran Beckett, *Called to Action*, Fount – a guide to communicating the faith by means of social action in the community.

Reference books

Ask at your local library for:

Benn's Media Directory
Willings Press Guide
Blue Book of British Broadcasting
UK Christian Handbook, MARC Europe – for detailed information on Christian organizations in the UK.

Useful addresses

ADMINISTRY, 69 Sandridge Road, St Albans, Hertfordshire AL1 4AG. Church administration specialists, who organize events to enthuse and train administrators of all kinds, and publish resource papers to share the best practices and ideas between churches.

Scripture Union Training Unit, 26–30 Heathcoat Street, Nottingham NG1 3AA. Runs training courses in evangelism, children's work, urban work and church administration.

Christmas Cracker, Oasis West Midlands, Cornerstone House, 5 Ethel Street, Birmingham B2 4BG. Organizers of the Radio Cracker project.

Evangelical Alliance, Whitfield House, 186 Kennington Park Road, London SE11 4BT.

March For Jesus, PO Box 39, Sunbury-on-Thames, Middlesex TW16 6PP.

The Church of England, Press & Broadcasting Department, Church House, London SW1P 3NZ. Runs courses to help churches improve communications.

The Church of Scotland's Department of Communication, 121 George Street, Edinburgh EH2 4YN. Provides training opportunities for those who wish to develop communication strategies for their congregation.

It is worth contacting the head office of your own denomination, or church grouping, to see what advice is available on publicity. The Church of England, for example, has a network of Diocesan Communication Officers to assist local churches.

The Media Awareness Project, 24 Tufton Street, London SW1P 3RB. Ecumenical project founded to increase awareness of the media and its effects, including evaluating its 'underlying values' from a Christian viewpoint.

The Institute of Public Relations is the professional body for PR practitioners. It has produced a series of Guidelines and Recommended Practice papers, and a leaflet on PR as a career. Details from the IPR, The Old Trading House, 15 Northburgh Street, London EC1V 0PR.

For Christians who are interested or involved in local braodcasting, the Churches Advisory Council for Local Broadcasting offers support, advice and an annual conference. Details from PO Box 124 Westcliff-on-Sea, Essex SS0 0QU.

Organizations involved in broadcasting and video

Churches Media Trust, Church House, North Hinksey, Oxford OX2 0NB.

CTVC, Hillside Studios, Merry Hill Road, Bushey, Watford, Hertfordshire WD2 1DR.

CVG Television, First House, Sutton Street, Birmingham B1 1PE.

International Films, The Coach House, 55 Drayton Green, London W13 0JD.

Trans World Radio, 45 London Road, Biggleswade, Bedfordshire SG18 8ED.

United Christian Broadcasters, Cauldron Buildings, Caledonia Road, Stoke-on-Trent ST4 2DN.

Vision Broadcasting Ministries, Shaftesbury Centre, Percy Street, Swindon SN2 2AZ.

Publicity materials

Materials to improve the impact of general church publicity are available from:

Bible Lands Trading, PO Box 50, High Wycombe, Buckinghamshire HP15 7QU.

Christian Publicity Organisation, Garcia Estate, Canterbury Road, Worthing, West Sussex BN13 1BW.

Church News Service, 37B New Cavendish Street, London W1M 8JR.

Challenge Literature Fellowship, Revenue Buildings, Chapel Road, Worthing, West Sussex BN11 1BQ.

Release Nationwide, Manchester City Mission, Peter House, 6 Oxford Street, Manchester M1 5AN. Release also produce *Say Something Simple*, a manual on church communications sent to subscribers in instalments.

Posters

Christian Publicity Organisation, Garcia Estate, Canterbury Road, Worthing, West Sussex BN13 1BW.

Gospel Posters, 8 Manstone Lane, Sidmouth, Devon EX10 9TS.

Scripture Gift Mission, Radstock House, 3 Eccleston Street, London SW1W 9LZ.

St Paul Multimedia Productions, Middle Green, Slough SL3 6BS.

Victory Tracts and Posters, Portland Road, London SE25 4PN.

Telephone service

Message Christian Telephone Service, 6 Darnley Road, Woodford Green, Essex IG8 9HU.

Signposting services

Automobile Association: Telephone 0800 393 808.
RAC Motoring Services: Telephone 0800 234 810.

The Shaftesbury Society, 18–20 Kingston Road, London SW19 1JZ has produced 'Love in Action', an action pack for churches to help them consider their role in the community. It includes worksheets, information sheets, Bible study outlines and case studies.

Appendix I

Job specification for communications officer

This is an outline job specification, which can be amended for use in a wide range of denominations.

Main roles

To publicize the church to the surrounding community.

To ensure information of importance/interest to church members is communicated efficiently to them.

Specific responsibilities

External communications

To keep the local media informed of church activities and special events.

To ensure that external posterboards are attractive, up-to-date and communicate relevant messages.

To organize the production and delivery of the church's external newsletter, and the production of other publicity material identified as needed by the church.

Monitor the effectiveness of the church's external communications, and make recommendations on how these can be improved, including the use of new communications methods.

Internal communications

To organize the production of all internal church publications, including the weekly noticesheet and quarterly magazine.

To oversee all internal church displays/posterboards, and ensure that they are looking presentable and up-to-date.

To monitor the effectiveness of internal communications, and make recommendations on how these can be improved.

Authority

The postholder is responsible to the minister for carrying out the above roles.

He/she is expected to recruit a team of helpers to carry out specific tasks within the above, but remains responsible for these tasks.

The postholder will be asked to give regular reports on his/her activities.

He/she will agree a budget for communications activities at the beginning of each financial year.

Postholder profile

Essential characteristics

He/she must:
- be a committed church member.
- be able to communicate well, in writing and in

public speaking.
- have a knowledge of all church activities, as well as the church's links with other national and local organizations and churches.
- be able to devote time to the role. Unlikely to have another major responsibility in the church.
- be a good organizer and administrator.
- have access to a typewriter or word processor.

Beneficial characteristics

He/she should:
- be able to be contacted during the day by the media.
- be able to take photographs for use in displays, presentations, and publications.
- have a knowledge of design.

Age/health

The postholder should be in good health, as he/she will often need to work accurately to tight deadlines.

Note: This is an honorary post, for which no salary is paid.

Appendix II

An outline communications survey

The questionnaire set out below is an outline for you to modify for your own church. Essentially, the questions are designed to encourage churchgoers to think about how well they are being kept in touch with the life of the church.

The responses should enable you to obtain an impression of how well-informed people feel they are, and from where they get their information. The categories will, of course, need to be adjusted for each church.

Further conversations, in small groups or individually, would be required to discover the types of information best communicated by each method. A questionnaire longer than the one outlined below might get a poor response because it would take too long to complete.

ANY CHURCH, ANYTOWN COMMUNICATIONS SURVEY

We would like your help in carrying out a survey of communications within the church. We want to ensure that everyone feels fully involved and knows what is going on.

We would be grateful if you could please take five minutes to complete this questionnaire, and return it to (named person) next Sunday. You do not have to add your name, but this would be helpful in case we would like to discuss your suggestions with you.

The information we receive from you and other church-goers will be used to decide how we can improve the way information is communicated within the church. We will let you know the results of this survey, and the ideas which come from it. Thank you for your co-operation.

Please circle the choice which indicates your reply.

1 How well informed do you feel about:

- this church's regular services?
    Very well/well/poor/very poor

- this church's regular activities?
    Very well/well/poor/very poor

- this church's special events?
    Very well/well/poor/very poor

- this church's role in the parish?
    Very well/well/poor/very poor

2 Please give your views on each of the following types of communication (Circle your reply).

- Church magazine.
As a source of information, I find this:
    Very useful/useful/unhelpful/very unhelpful

Please briefly explain your reply.

How could it be improved?

- **Weekly noticesheet.**

As a source of information, I find this:
    Very useful/useful/unhelpful/very unhelpful

Please briefly explain your reply.

How could it be improved?

- **Noticeboards inside the church.**

As a source of information, I find these:
    Very useful/useful/unhelpful/very unhelpful

Please briefly explain your reply.

How could they be improved?

- **Special displays.**

As a source of information, I find these:
    Very useful/useful/unhelpful/very unhelpful

Please briefly explain your reply.

How could they be improved?

- **Announcements in church.**

As a source of information, I find these:
    Very useful/useful/unhelpful/very unhelpful

Please briefly explain your reply.

How could they be improved?

- **Church business meetings.**

As a source of information, I find these:
    Very useful/useful/unhelpful/very unhelpful

Please briefly explain your reply.

How could they be improved?

- Letters from the minister.
As a source of information, I find these:
    Very useful/useful/unhelpful/very unhelpful

Please briefly explain your reply.

How could they be improved?

- Religious publications
Do you read any religious magazines or newsletters, including those produced by Christian charities and missionary groups?

              Yes/No

If you do, which are they?

Please indicate briefly any other forms of communication which you find particularly helpful, and why.

3 Do you have any other suggestions about how communications could be improved. Please write them down as briefly as possible. We would like the opportunity to discuss these further with you.

Thank you for completing this survey.

OUT NOW!

Princess Brides: A Royal Baby

3 BOOKS IN ONE

Amy Ruttan · Catherine Mann · Jennie Lucas

Available at
millsandboon.co.uk

MILLS & BOON

OUT NOW!

3 BOOKS IN ONE

- ROMANCE ON DUTY -

UNDERCOVER

CINDI MYERS JO LEIGH SARAH M. ANDERSON

Available at
millsandboon.co.uk

MILLS & BOON

OUT NOW!

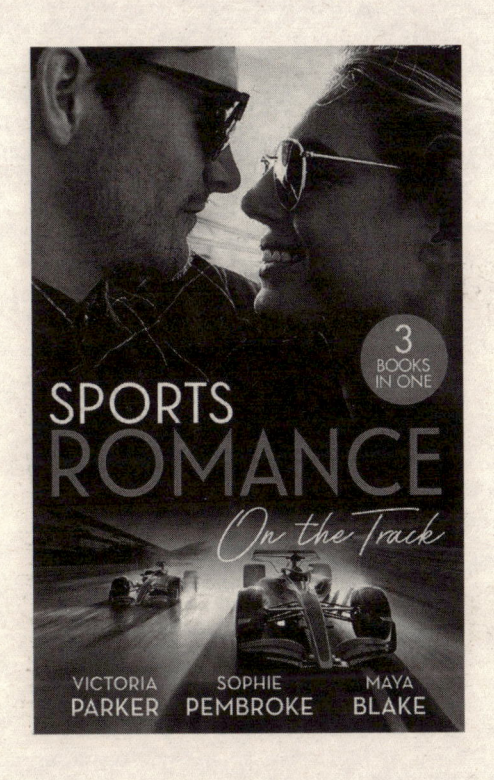

SPORTS ROMANCE
On the Track

VICTORIA PARKER · SOPHIE PEMBROKE · MAYA BLAKE

3 BOOKS IN ONE

Available at
millsandboon.co.uk

MILLS & BOON

OUT NOW!

Opposites Attract: Rancher's Attraction

3 BOOKS IN ONE

MAISEY YATES
JOANNE ROCK
JOSS WOOD

Available at
millsandboon.co.uk

MILLS & BOON